painting murals
fast & easy

TERRENCE and THEODORE TSE

painting murals
fast & easy

* *21 designs for walls or canvas you can paint with a sponge*

NORTH LIGHT BOOKS

Cincinnati, Ohio
www.artistsnetwork.com

"Clearwater"

A B O U T   T H E   A U T H O R S

Terrence and Theodore Tse are twin brothers whose art education began during their high school years. They each received scholarships to continue their formal art training, but military service intervened and college was deferred. Nevertheless, they have enjoyed success as freelance artists and have participated in art shows and gallery exhibitions. They spent eight years as lead production artists and managers for a company that reproduces handpainted artworks for major retail outlets. During this time they learned how to paint in a realistic, representational style with speed, accuracy and efficiency. They developed their own innovative techniques for using acrylic paints and common household sponges to achieve large-scale paintings quickly and easily. These techniques have been applied to mural painting in this, their first book for North Light. Terry and Ted Tse reside in Peachtree City, Georgia.

Other fine North Light Books are available from your local bookstore, art supply store or direct from the publisher.

09 08 07 06 05   5 4 3 2 1

Library of Congress Cataloging-in-Publication Data

Tse, Terrence
    Painting murals fast & easy / Terrence and Theodore Tse.
        p. cm.
    Includes index.
    ISBN 1-58180-573-X (pbk. : alk. paper)
  1. Mural painting and decoration--Technique. I. Title: Painting murals fast and easy. II. Tse, Theodore. III. Title.
    ND2550.T74 2005
    751.4--dc22
                             2004024757

Edited by Kathy Kipp
Interior designed by Stanard Design Partners
Photographed by Christine Polomsky
Production coordinated by Kristen Heller

F·W PUBLICATIONS, INC.

Metric Conversion Chart		
To convert	**to**	**multiply by**
Inches	Centimeters	2.54
Centimeters	Inches	0.4
Feet	Centimeters	30.5
Centimeters	Feet	0.03
Yards	Meters	0.9
Meters	Yards	1.1
Sq. Inches	Sq. Centimeters	6.45
Sq. Centimeters	Sq. Inches	0.16
Sq. Feet	Sq. Meters	0.09
Sq. Meters	Sq. Feet	10.8
Sq. Yards	Sq. Meters	0.8
Sq. Meters	Sq. Yards	1.2
Pounds	Kilograms	0.45
Kilograms	Pounds	2.2
Ounces	Grams	28.3
Grams	Ounces	0.035

DEDICATION

From Ted:
To my twin, Lun.
To my elder brother, William.
To Mousey and Sunlun.

From Terry:
To my twin, Chui.
To my son, Sunlun, and his mother, Stephanie L. Pilbeam.

A special dedication from both of us to our entire Tseh family:
William, Kenneth, Tyler, Jenny, Julie, Francis, Fulton, Wayland,
and Lana F. Tseh and Wong C. Tseh.

ACKNOWLEDGMENTS

Thanks to the expert services provided by the great staff at North Light Books,
and especially to Kathy Kipp for her support.

To Michael King for sharing his years of artistic insights.

To David and Ruth Mabry for their understanding.

To Tim Gassler for being a quality friend.

Table of Contents

introduction

Murals are one of today's most popular and creative ways to decorate the walls of your home. No other painting technique puts such a unique and personal stamp on your surroundings, or brings such joy and satisfaction to both the artist and the viewer.

In the past, painting a mural on a wall in your home meant spending many hours in preparation, measuring, enlarging and copying a pattern or drawing, assembling just the right brushes and paints, buying special equipment, painting the mural with slow, deliberate strokes, wiping off mistakes and starting again....

In this book you will discover a new and innovative way to paint murals quickly and easily using acrylic paints and common household sponges. No brushes needed! No experience required!

Painting with sponges is downright fun—and it frees you from the fear and frustration of making mistakes. Don't like what you've just painted? Spray the area with water and remove it with a clean sponge. It's just that easy.

The sponges used to paint the murals in this book are the inexpensive cellulose ones you can find in any grocery, hardware or home improvement store. We also used a natural sea sponge to achieve some interesting effects, such as layers of colorful foliage on trees and bushes.

To clean the paint from your sponges, just squeeze them out in a bucket of water. The paints we used in this book are all acrylics, which are water-based, have no odor, and can be thinned or removed with plain water before they dry.

The mural painting techniques in this book will allow you to paint a mural almost anywhere in your home. You may paint directly on a wall or ceiling that has been basecoated with standard household latex paint. Or, if you want the freedom and flexibility to take the mural with you when you move, you can paint your mural on regular artist's canvas that comes in all sizes at your local art and craft store.

Painting your mural on canvas also offers several creative and attractive display options. You can:
• adhere the canvas flat to a wall using wallpaper paste;
• mount the canvas on wooden stretcher bars and hang it from picture frame hooks;
• fold over the top edge and hang from a decorative rod;
• frame the mural with picture molding from the home center.

In this book, you will learn many simple techniques for achieving a wide variety of painted effects you can use in any mural, from scenic landscapes to oceanfront beaches to floral still lifes and more. You will see how easy it is to speed-paint clouds and skies, sandy shorelines, sun-dappled palm trees, tropical flowers, serene rivers and thundering waterfalls, plus grassy hills, tree-shaded streams, fields of colorful flowers, and so much more.

None of the murals demonstrated in this book took longer than two hours to paint! Sponges allow you to cover a large amount of space in a matter of minutes. They also let you shade and highlight quickly to achieve depth and realism.

Try your hand at mixing and matching the ideas you see in these pages to create your own unique mural, and then discover how much fun it is to paint with sponges!

—Terry and Ted Tse

"Bouquet in Bronze"

materials & basic sponge painting techniques

The materials used to paint all the murals in this book are shown here. These items can be purchased at your local home center and craft supply store. In this chapter, you will see how easy it is to sponge-paint many different elements found in murals of all kinds, from landscapes to ocean scenes to still lifes. All of the following techniques are used to paint the murals in this book. Try them out on a piece of canvas before you paint your mural to get the feel and rhythm of working with a sponge.

Manufactured cellulose sponge
Better known simply as a household cleaning sponge, this sponge is a cellulose composite with breadlike pores and texture. It measures 7½″ x 4″ x 2″ (19.1cm x 10.2cm x 5.1cm).

Natural sea sponge
This type of sponge is grown and cultivated. Generally, the sea sponge has deep tunneling pores and a coral-like surface. The natural surface texture is ideal for random effects.

Water bucket
A small one or two gallon bucket of water will be needed to rinse out the sponge.

Spray bottle of water
Use to moisten the canvas or wall, keep your paint wet, and thin the paint if needed.

Rubber gloves
Sponge painting requires physical contact with paint, so you may want to use thin disposable rubber gloves.

Paper towels
For wiping your hands and cleaning up drips.

Steel ruler
A steel ruler or straight edge may be used to produce straight cuts when dividing a sponge into thirds.

Scissors
Scissors may also be used to cut sponges into smaller sizes.

Pencil
Use to lightly sketch your design on a wall or canvas.

Foam plate
An inexpensive foam plate can serve as a palette for your paints.

Craft knife
A utility or craft knife can be used to cut a large sponge into manageable sizes.

Eraser
Use a rubber eraser to remove pencil lines after painting.

Acrylic paints
These waterbased paints can be found at any craft store and come in a wide variety of colors.

How to Cut and Hold the Sponge

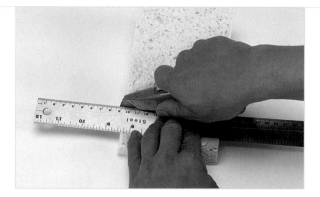

1 Press down on a steel ruler or other straight edge and cut straight down through the sponge.

2 You can get three manageable sponges out of one large one.

3 This is the widest side of the sponge. Use this side for broad strokes and washes, and to get a lot of paint on quickly.

4 The narrow or vertical side of the sponge is the side used most often when painting on walls or canvas.

5 The sponge may be squeezed into various widths to paint small areas. Shown here is what is called a "thin crunch."

6 The very edge can be used to make thin brushlike lines and crisp edges.

Loading the Sponge with Paint

1 To paint large areas quickly, load the entire face by pressing the sponge into a large puddle of paint.

2 Loading just the top half will keep the sponge from getting too saturated with paint.

3 Load just the corner of the sponge to paint small areas and to make brushlike strokes.

4 To make thin lines such as twigs and branches, carefully load just the very top edge.

5 A sponge can also be double loaded on the corners to apply two colors at once, which allows you to shade or highlight with one stroke.

Getting Started with the Sponge

1 To wash on a smooth, flat color, use circular motions to apply the paint. Continue spreading the paint randomly until all streak marks are worked away.

2 Parallel strokes have a number of uses, ranging from skies to water to grass.

3 Crisscross the sponge in random motions to make grass clumps and leaves.

4 Wiggling the sponge helps to spread the paint in a more controlled manner than a wash.

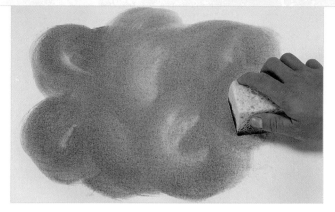

5 To achieve this stippled, dotlike pattern, use a natural sea sponge to lightly dab on the paint. This is an easy way to paint foliage on trees and bushes.

6 Here is how the same dabbing motion looks with a regular cellulose sponge. Its porous surface is great for adding texture.

Achieving Brushlike Effects

Dry-sponging is similar to a "dry-brushing" technique, where paint is sparingly loaded onto a slightly damp sponge and applied with light pressure so that the marks are somewhat broken and the painting surface or undercolor shows through.

Impasto is a technique of applying paint in thick and heavy applications so that the paint creates a tactile surface. Caution: Paint applied this thickly takes a longer time to dry and cure.

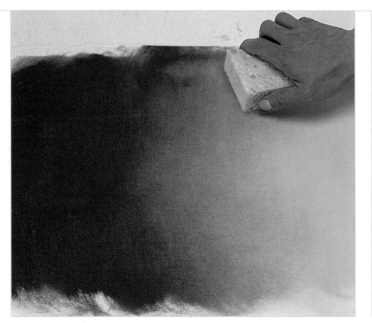

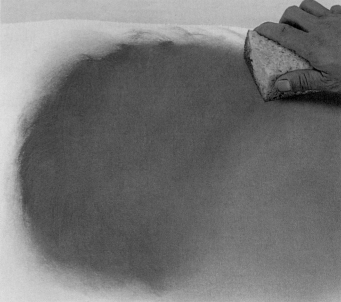

Blending different colors into each other while they are wet is called painting *wet-into-wet*. This technique creates smooth gradations of color and creamy middle tones, and is great for painting skies at sunset, for example.

Glazing is a technique whereby colors are glazed over a previously applied hue that is completely dry. You may use a different color to achieve middle tones or to change the first layer of color entirely. Glazing the same color over a first layer can intensify the color, making it deeper and richer.

Ocean Waves

1 Load the top edge of the sponge with white paint. Turn the sponge so the white edge faces downward and crunch the sponge to achieve a slight curve to the edge. Create rolling waves by dabbing and drawing uneven curves with a wiggly motion.

2 Turn the sponge over to the clean side and soften and blend out from the top of the wave, pulling upward toward the horizon. Note that the water is darker just underneath the white crest of the wave.

White Clouds

1 Load the top portion of the narrow side of the sponge with white paint.

2 Dab and shape the upper area of the puffy white clouds with the edge of the sponge.

3 Blend downward to soften. Repeat steps 1, 2 and 3 to layer thicker and more opaque areas of clouds to build volume and mass. Be sure to leave thinner areas where the blue sky color shows through.

4 If your clouds are over water in your mural, use the edge of your sponge and white paint to streak horizontal clouds just above the water. Turn your sponge over to the clean side and wipe over these streaks to soften and blend a little bit.

Palm Fronds

1 Load the top edge of the sponge with dark green paint. Draw the stems with the edge of the sponge.

2 Pull out leaves from the stem using a dry-sponge technique. Leave streak lines to indicate details.

3 For the middle frond, pull out leaves from both sides of the stem. For airier leaves, use less paint on your sponge.

Grass

1 Load the top edge of the sponge sparingly with green paint as shown.

2 Turn the sponge so the paint edge is downward. Pull up streaks in random curves and lengths, leaving plenty of open spaces.

Flowering Shrubs

1   Load a household or natural sea sponge with a dark green undercolor. Dab in a rounded shape, leaving the edges open and airy looking.

2   Load the sponge with a medium green and dab in lighter leaves, but don't cover the undercolor completely.

3   Load the sponge with a bright red, crunch it into a curve, and dab in red flowers here and there.

4   Pick up a little white on your sponge, crunch it into a tighter curve, and highlight the red flowers wet-into-wet. Avoid the areas where the shrub is in shade.

Tree Trunks

1 Load the edge of the sponge with a dark brown undercolor and draw in the main trunk and the branches.

2 Load a medium brown onto the edge of the sponge. Dab and dry-sponge areas to create a bark texture.

3 Load a bit of white onto the edge of the sponge, crunch the sponge into a tight curve and highlight one side of the trunk and branches where the light is strongest.

Tree Foliage

1 Draw in the trunk and branches as shown on page 19. Load either a household sponge or a natural sea sponge with a dark green undercolor. Dab in the first layer of foliage, leaving many open areas where the trunk and branches can show through.

2 Load the sponge with a middle value yellow-green and dab in the next layer of foliage, again leaving open spaces.

3 Load the sponge with white and dab in highlights where the sunlight hits the leaves. Don't highlight where the tree is shaded.

Waterfall

1 Wash in a mixture of Raw Umber and Thalo Blue for the horizontal water at the top of the falls. Wash in vertical streaks under the precipice and blend with the clean side of the sponge.

2 Load White onto the edge of the sponge and apply short horizontal strokes at the top to show turbulent water.

3 Dry-sponge vertical white streaks along the face of the falling water, allowing the gray-blue under-color to show through.

4 Blend the vertical streaks a little and re-establish the top edge of the falls with the brightest white. Do not cover the undercolor entirely.

5 Dab and stipple on white foam at the bottom of the falls. Don't overdo—keep it airy and light.

Rocks and Boulders

1 Load a household sponge with a deep blue-gray undercolor. Use short drags of the sponge in random directions to place the undercolor.

2 Establish rock faces and planes using short drags of the sponge loaded with a medium shade of dark cream.

3 Load a corner of the sponge with burnt sienna and add a medium tone to the rocks here and there.

4 Highlight the upper faces of the rocks with a light cream tone.

Water Cascading over Rocks

1 Sponge-paint a grouping of rocks and boulders as shown on page 22. To create the water they sit in, start with a wash of bluish undercolor. Then load the edge of the sponge with white and place short random strokes around the base of the rocks.

2 Still with white, use the corner of the sponge to draw rivulets of water spilling over the rocks. Stipple on foam where the water splashes up against the rocks. A natural sea sponge is good for stippling splashing water.

Autumn Foliage

1 Load a natural sea sponge with dark green and dab in the undercolor.

2 Load medium green onto the sponge and apply a layer of lighter leaves. Let the dark green show through on the undersides.

3 Dab in some lighter leaves at the top of the tree and a few other areas with yellow ochre.

4 To highlight the fall leaves, dab on some bright yellow, leaving the undersides dark.

5 Use burnt sienna to shade the undersides of the yellow leaves. Draw in some dark brown tree branches among the foliage using the edge of a household sponge.

Storm Clouds

1 Load a household sponge with a dark gray-purple and wiggle the sponge in horizontal bands of undercolor. Soften the upper cloud by blending out with the clean side of the sponge. Keep the underside of this cloud more defined.

2 Pull out streaks of the undercolor from the main cloud decks. Make sure your hand motions are horizontal.

3 Load the top portion of the sponge with white and dab in white clouds along the tops of the storm clouds. Soften and blend. Reapply more white in a few areas to strengthen the clouds and add mass and volume.

4 Use the edge of the sponge to streak white horizontal under-clouds. Soften and blend with the clean side of the sponge.

Glass Vase

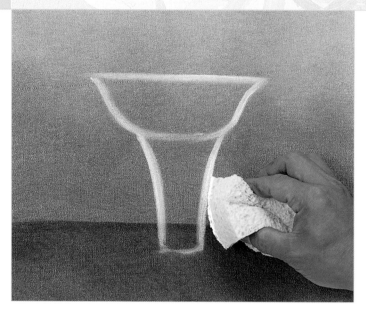

1   Load the edge of a household sponge with white. Crunch the sponge into a curve, and outline the shape of the vase.

2   Pull white inward from the outline, then blend and fade out to give the illusion of a rounded shape.

3   Streak vertical white lines in the base for reflections, then blend and soften in some areas. Load white onto the corner of the sponge and draw a design in the bowl that looks like cut crystal. To create the reflection on the table in front of the vase, wiggle the sponge out from the base at an angle, then blend a little.

Roses and Leaves

1. Load the edge of a household sponge with a deep green. Block in the leaf shapes using the corner of the sponge to sketch the serrated edges.

2. Load a lighter green plus a bit of yellow on the sponge and draw in the veins and highlights.

3. Block in the basic shape of the rose with a dark magenta undercolor. Apply the paint rather thickly to give texture and definition to the petals.

4. With white on your sponge, use a combination of wet-into-wet and impasto techniques to stroke in the layers of petals. Do not cover the dark undercolor entirely—let those petals show for shading and depth.

PART ONE

6 step-by-step
mural demonstrations

Color Tips

The colors used in all the following step-by-step demonstrations are mixes made with waterbased acrylic paints. You can find hundreds of acrylic colors in convenient 2-oz. (57g) bottles at your local craft supply store. The color charts at the beginning of each demonstration are meant to help you match the colors you buy as closely as possible to the colors used in painting each mural. With so many colors available, you should have no trouble finding the ones you need. If you prefer, you can make your own color palette to suit your home, or change the colors used in these murals to ones you like better.

Now let's use the sponge-painting techniques you have learned so far to create gorgeous murals for your home.

The first mural demonstration, titled "Clearwater," is a warm and inviting beach scene, and uses four techniques you learned about on pages 15-17: ocean waves, white puffy clouds, palm fronds and grasses.

The second mural demonstration, "Morning View," is a quiet country roadway in the glow of dawn. Here you'll see the techniques for painting flowering shrubs, tree trunks, and foliage.

The third mural is called "Lavender Field," a lovely green valley dotted with hundreds of colorful flowers, all painted with a double-loaded sponge to create highlights and shadows in one stroke.

The fourth mural, "Waterfall," is an impressive and beautiful setting of thundering falls amid flowering trees. The painting techniques include a translucent waterfall, rocks and boulders, water cascading over rocks, and trees with colorful foliage.

"Edge of Paradise" evokes a tropical getaway in the light of a blazing sunset, and you'll learn an easy technique for creating storm clouds.

Finally, "Red Roses" is a classic still life of a dozen roses in all shades of red, pink and orange. Here you'll find techniques for painting a glass vase as well as rose petals and leaves.

"Morning View"

clearwater

* Inspired by the white sand beaches of Florida's Gulf Coast, this painting invites you to relax, stay awhile, smell the salt air and feel the warm sand under your feet. As the gentle waves roll in toward the beach, the water changes color from deep blue to blue-green, and tall palms shade the colorful tropical flowers. In this demonstration, you'll see how to paint ocean blue water, rolling waves and soft sand beaches.

Color Mixes

1 Light Blue
2 Cream
3 Deep Blue Sky
4 Deep Water Blue
5 Sea Green
6 Dark Sand
7 Dark Brown
8 Titanium White
9 Medium Brown
10 Medium Light Brown
11 Lightest Brown
12 Dark Foliage Green
13 Raw Sienna
14 Highlight Green
15 Red Accent
16 Magenta
17 Purple
18 Light Pink
19 Dark Blue-Gray

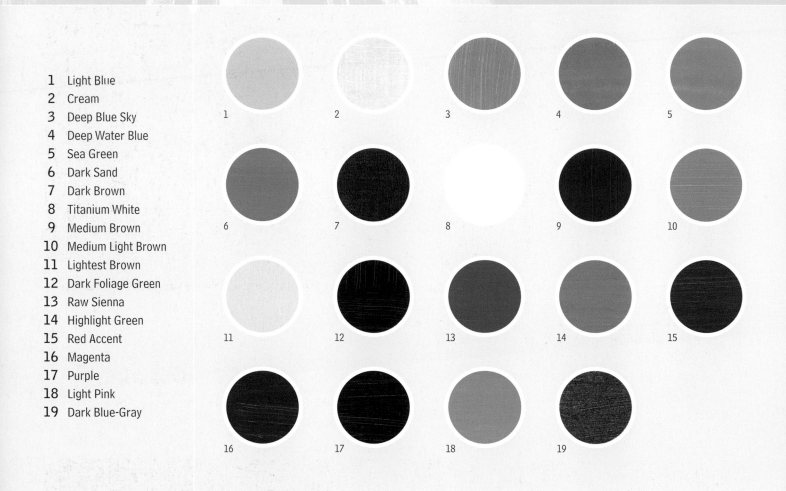

Sky, Water and Sand

1 Lightly pencil in the horizon line and the placement of the two palm tree trunks. Use a spray bottle of clean water to lightly mist the surface. Wash a thin layer of Light Blue over the sky area and down into the distant water area. Wash a thin layer of Cream across the bottom for the sand beach.

2 Wash Deep Blue Sky over the top part of the sky to deepen the sky color.

3 Load the sponge with Deep Water Blue and wash in the water area from the horizon line down to where it meets the sandy beach. Keep your hand motions horizontal.

4 Add a bit of green and a touch of white to the Deep Water Blue color to make Sea Green. Layer in this color for the lighter, shallower part of the water closer to the beach.

Clouds and Waves

5 Add a bit of Burnt Sienna and Raw Sienna to the Cream sand color to make Dark Sand. Mottle in some darker areas in the sand.

6 Add Raw Umber to the Dark Sand color to make Dark Brown. Mottle in some dips and low places in the sand.

7 Begin painting the clouds from top to bottom with Titanium White thinned with a little water. Start with the larger, bright white masses and keep the brightest white toward the tops of the clouds.

8 Sponge in the middle decks of clouds with Titanium White that is a bit thicker than in step 7.

9 Load the top edge of the sponge with Titanium White and streak in the lowest clouds above the horizon line. Keep these streaks short and randomly placed here and there.

10 Load the very top edge of the sponge with Titanium White and streak in distant waves in the water at the horizon line.

11 Again using Titanium White, turn the sponge so the white edge is facing downward and wiggle in some white waves coming in to shore. Flip the sponge over to the clean side and blend out the upper edges of the waves.

12 Use the same White and the same wiggling and blending out technique for the waves breaking over the sandy beach.

13 With Titanium White, mottle in some highlights in the beach area to create high spots in the sand.

Palm Trees

14 With Medium Brown on the corner of the sponge, draw in the palm tree trunks starting at the top and stroking downward.

15 Map out the palm frond stems with a Medium Brown undercolor, using the corner of the sponge. Drag leaves out from the stems using a dry-sponge technique.

16 With Medium Light Brown, highlight the trunks with short, slightly curved, horizontal strokes using the very edge of the sponge.

17 With Lightest Brown, highlight the trunks in a hit-and-miss way, keeping the highlights on one side only.

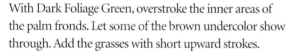

19 Highlight some of the tops of the palm fronds with Raw Sienna, using the dry-sponge technique.

18 With Dark Foliage Green, overstroke the inner areas of the palm fronds. Let some of the brown undercolor show through. Add the grasses with short upward strokes.

20 Apply the final highlight on the palm fronds with Highlight Green just on the tops to show sunlight hitting them.

21 Mix equal parts Burnt Sienna and Naphthol Red Light to get the Red Accent color. Add reddish accents to the palm fronds here and there on the undersides.

Grasses and Flowers

22 Begin the flowers under the palm trees with Magenta dabbed on with a natural sea sponge.

23 Add the darker value Purple here and there with the sea sponge.

24 Highlight the flowers with Light Pink in the areas where the sunlight would be hitting them.

25 Dab in a few touches of Raw Sienna to indicate dried-up leaves and flowers.

Critique

Step back from your work and take a critical look at all parts of your painting. Are there any areas that need a little bit more attention to detail? Are the colors balanced and harmonious? In this painting, the foliage area needed a bit more shading where the grasses grow up out of the sand. A Dark Blue-Gray mixed from Thalo Blue and Raw Umber was dabbed on to deepen those areas and subdue the colors a bit so the center of attention would remain on the clouds and water.

morning view

* In this mural, a quiet country road leads you into the distance. The trees are set aglow by the soft colors of the morning sunrise, and the shadows are still deep and dark. Here you will learn how to paint grassy fields, flowering shrubs, distant trees, and how the rosy light of dawn colors the wispy clouds above.

Color Mixes

1 Blue Sky
2 Pink Sky
3 Grass Undercolor
4 Burnt Sienna
5 Pink Clouds
6 Titanium White
7 Medium Grass Green
8 Deep Grass Green
9 Grass Highlight
10 Light Grass Highlight
11 Dark Shadow Green
12 Deep Burnt Sienna
13 Dark Brown
14 Dark Green Undercolor
15 Yellow Highlight
16 Magenta
17 Purple
18 Dark Olive
19 Dark Tree Green
20 Red Accent
21 Tree Trunk Highlight
22 Greenish-Cream

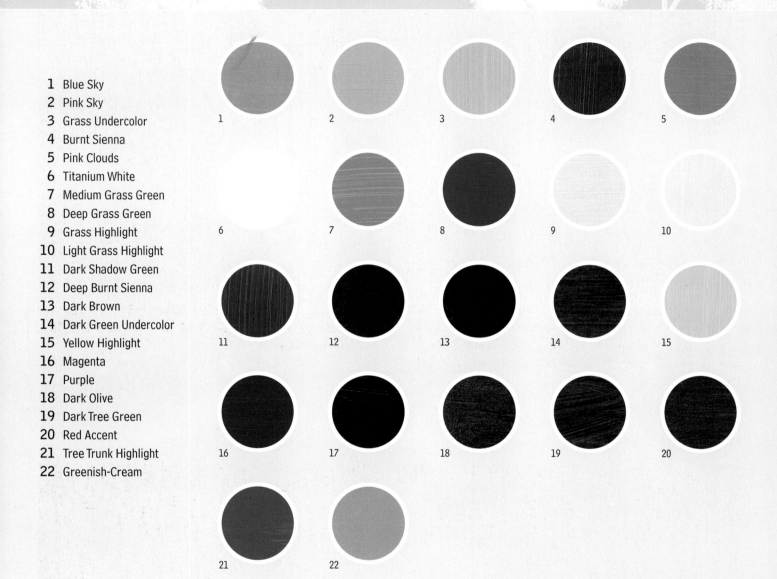

Sky, Grass and Roadway

1 Lightly pencil in the horizon line and the placement of the trees, shrubs and roadway. Use a spray bottle of clean water to lightly mist the surface. Wash a thin layer of Blue Sky over the sky area, starting at the top and working about a third of the way down.

2 Wash in a thin layer of Pink Sky under the blue sky area, ending at the horizon line. This gives the pinkish hue to the sunrise colors.

3 Load the sponge with Grass Undercolor and wash in the grassy areas from the horizon line on down, avoiding the roadway.

4 Load the sponge with Burnt Sienna and wash in the roadway. Do not be concerned if the edges of the road are a bit ragged; the flowering shrubs will cover this.

Clouds and Grasses

5 Add a bit of Raw Sienna and Magenta to the Pink Sky color to deepen it, making the Pink Clouds mix. Streak in some cirrus clouds that are pink with the morning sunrise.

6 Use Titanium White to add puffy clouds to the blue sky area, blending out the edges to soften. Add even softer blended-out clouds to the pink sky area.

7 With Medium Grass Green, paint the slightly darker layer of the grassy area. Use short, random strokes of the sponge in a mostly downward direction.

8 Add Deep Grass Green to the grassy areas for the shadows cast by the trees and bushes.

9 Load the sponge with Grass Highlight color and highlight the grass hit and miss in the medium green areas. Streak a thin yellow line along the horizon line using the same Grass Highlight color.

10 Add Titanium White plus a tiny bit of green to the Grass Highlight color to make Light Grass Highlight. Make short, choppy strokes of this highlight color in the lighter green areas.

11 Load Dark Shadow Green on the sponge and deepen the shadowy areas of the grass. Dab in random areas of this color into the light green areas as well, but don't overdo it.

12 Deepen the roadway color with Deep Burnt Sienna mottled into the undercolor. Don't cover the under-color completely, and pull your sponge strokes in the direction the roadway is going.

Flowering Shrubs

13 Shade the road with Dark Brown where the flowering shrubs will cast their shadows. Blend out the edges of the shadows into the roadway color to soften.

14 Begin placing in the flowering shrubs with a first layer of Dark Green Undercolor. Pinch or crunch the sponge to shape the three large shrubs along the left side of the road, and dab in a row of low bushes along the right side.

15 With Yellow Highlight, dab in strong highlights on the three large shrubs, and a few highlights on the lower bushes.

16 Load the top edge of the sponge with Magenta and dab in the first layer of flowers on the shrubs. Let the yellow and green undercolors show through.

17 Dab on a few Purple flowers here and there on the large shrubs. On the small bushes on the right side, keep the purple color to the underside to act as shading.

18 Finally, dab a few Titanium White flowers mostly on the large shrubs, with a few on the smaller ones. Spark up the flower colors with a few more dabs of Magenta here and there on both sides of the roadway.

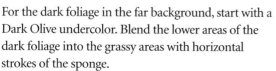

19 For the dark foliage in the far background, start with a Dark Olive undercolor. Blend the lower areas of the dark foliage into the grassy areas with horizontal strokes of the sponge.

20 Using your original pencil lines for placement, dab on Dark Tree Green for the tree foliage. Use the edge of your sponge to shape the trees, keeping the outer foliage areas light and airy.

Trees and Foliage

21 Load the sponge with the Grass Undercolor you used in step 3. Dab in lighter green foliage on the sunlit areas of the trees. In this painting, the morning sun is coming from the left.

22 Dab in Burnt Sienna in some areas of the trees on the left and over most of the smaller tree in the background to add warm tones to the foliage.

23 Add a bit of Red Accent color to the roadway sides of the two smaller trees in the background to pick up a bit of reflection of the road color.

24 Highlight all the trees here and there with Greenish-Cream. Draw in the tree trunks with Dark Brown on the edge of the sponge. Add a little Titanium White to this Dark Brown to make Tree Trunk Highlight color. Where the sunlight is hitting the trunks, stroke the highlight color in a narrow vertical streak on one side of each trunk.

Critique

Step back from your work and take a critical look at all parts of your painting. Are there any areas that need a little bit more attention to detail? Are the colors balanced and harmonious? In this painting, the tallest part of the tree on the left is shaped like a snowman's hat! Dab in a bit more of the Dark Tree Green to blend out that odd shape. Deepen the shadows under the trees and bushes to give more of an early-morning contrast. The foreground flowering shrub has too much of a round ball shape. Break up that roundness with more of the Dark Shadow Green, then re-highlight with a lighter green. The topmost shrub is hitting right at the horizon line, so add a bit more light green to the horizon to better set the shrub into the foreground.

lavender field

In this mural, a field dotted with colorful wildflowers leads into a quiet green valley. The distant hills and mountains are suggested with pinks and purples softened with misty, low-lying fog. The trees are a mix of evergreens and deciduous, leading one to feel that this is an undisturbed mountain valley and a truly natural landscape. This project will show you how to paint velvety green valleys, distant mountains, evergreens, and wildflowers of all colors.

Color Mixes

1 Light Sky Hue
2 Light Yellow-Green
3 Upper Sky Blue
4 Distant Mountain
   Lavender
5 Distant Mountain
   Pink
6 Dusty Mauve
7 Titanium White
8 Dark Tree Green
9 Medium Tree Green
10 Highlight Green
11 Burnt Sienna
12 Medium Grass Green
13 Yellow Grass
14 Tree Trunk Brown
15 Medium Tree Brown
16 Bright Tree Green
17 Light Green Highlight
18 Yellow Ochre
19 Raw Sienna
20 Cadmium Red
21 Rose Pink
22 Purple
23 Lemon Yellow
24 Light Grass Green

Sky and Green Valley

1 Lightly pencil in the lines of the distant hills and valleys, and the placement of the trees. Use a spray bottle of clean water to mist the surface lightly. Wash a thin layer of Light Sky Hue over the sky area starting at the top and letting it fade out into the middle ground area.

2 Wash in a thin layer of Light Yellow-Green for the valley and foreground fields, using curving horizontal strokes of the sponge to indicate the lay of the land. Come back in with more of this color to intensify the center of the valley and the edges of the field areas.

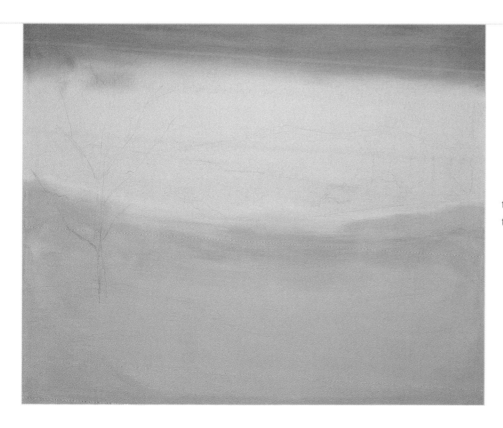

3 Load the sponge with Upper Sky Blue and wash in the darker sky area along the top, blending it down into the Light Sky Hue. Use horizontal strokes of the sponge.

Distant Mountains

4. Load the sponge with Distant Mountain Lavender and wash in the farthest distant mountains, using the top edge of the sponge to draw the shapes, following your pencil lines. Soften and blend out this color along the slopes.

5. Load the sponge with Distant Mountain Pink and draw in the lower hills, again using the edge of the sponge to follow the pencil lines. Blend out this color along the slopes of the hills.

6. Wash in the darker mountain on the left with Dusty Mauve, using the edge of the sponge to get the sweeping downward slopes of the mountainsides. Intensify the color in some areas to show low places and valleys. Turn the sponge over to the clean side to soften and blend.

Clouds and Trees

7 Begin adding in the clouds with Titanium White, using the edge of the sponge to draw the upper edge of the clouds. Soften and blend the lower areas into the blue sky. Wash in some very subtle white in the distant mountains to set them more into the background.

8 Load the sponge with thinned Dusty Mauve and wash in the reflected colors on the undersides of some of the clouds.

9 Using a natural sea sponge, dab in the distant trees with Dark Tree Green. While this color is still wet, take your household sponge and sweep some color out from under the trees onto the field area to create shadows and low places in the grass.

Field Grasses

10 Again using the natural sea sponge, load it with Medium Tree Green and add a layer of lighter foliage in some of the upper areas of the trees, leaving the lower areas in shade.

11 Load the natural sea sponge with Highlight Green and dab on a few lightest highlights in the very tops of the trees on both sides of the valley. Turn the sponge to a clean side and soften as you go.

12 Enrich the middle ground fields with washes of Burnt Sienna, starting in the background under the trees and working into the foreground. Turn the sponge over to the clean side and soften with sweeping motions, following the slight curve of the valley.

13 With Medium Grass Green, add shading and low spots in the field grasses. In the near foreground, block in the foliage using upward strokes with the edge of the sponge.

Foreground Tree

14 Block in the shadow where the foreground tree will be using Dark Tree Green. Mottle the shadow to show dappled sunlight coming through the leaves onto the ground beneath.

15 Add patches of Yellow Grass color here and there in the field and in the shadow area under the foreground tree.

16 Load the sponge with Tree Trunk Brown. Stroke in the main trunk and branches by crunching the sponge and using the edge to pull the trunk and branches upward.

17 Load the very edge of the sponge with Medium Tree Brown and highlight just the right sides of the trunk and branches. Use short, choppy strokes on the trunk, and smooth, vertical strokes on the branches.

Tree Foliage

18 Begin the first layer of foliage on the foreground tree with Dark Tree Green, leaving lots of open spaces. Use the corner of a household sponge in short, random-direction strokes.

19 Using the same sponge and stroke motion, add lighter foliage with Bright Tree Green, again leaving some open spaces.

20 Add the lightest leaves in areas where the sunlight would hit the tree using Light Green Highlight color.

21 Enrich the foliage color in a few places with a few dabs of Yellow Ochre.

22 Do the same in even fewer places with Raw Sienna.

23 Finish the foliage with a very few spots of Burnt Sienna to show dried leaves.

Wildflowers

24 Begin adding the wildflowers that dot the grassy fields. Load just the corner of a household sponge with Cadmium Red and start at the back of the field and work forward. The flowers are more sparse in the background; the main drifts are in the foreground. Dab in the flowers using the corner of the sponge with quick, random motions. There are many more flower colors to come, so leave lots of open spaces for now.

25 Clean out your sponge with water, squeeze out the excess, and load one corner with Rose Pink. Using the same technique as for the red flowers, dab in some pink flowers here and there. Place a few drifts in the back of the field. Load the other corner of the sponge with Titanium White and use a wet-into-wet technique to add lighter pink and white flowers.

26 To paint the purple flowers, double load the sponge with Purple on one corner and Titanium White on the other. Dab in some purple flowers, then change to the white corner of the sponge and go over the purple flowers to create lavender-colored flowers in some places. Concentrate these colors underneath the tree, with a few scattered out in the field area.

27 The yellow flowers are painted with a sponge that is double loaded into Lemon Yellow on one corner and Titanium White on the other. Dot in drifts of yellow flowers in the field and in the foreground. Top the foreground with yellow and white flowers.

28 Once the flowers are as you like them, come back in with Light Grass Green and stroke some foliage in among the flowers, using an upward motion.

Critique

Step back from your work and take a critical look at all parts of your painting. Are there any areas that need a little bit more attention to detail? Are the colors balanced and harmonious? In this painting, a few areas need some deeper shadowing using Dark Tree Green, including underneath the background foliage and the foreground tree, and also some areas along the right edge.

Add a few more low or shaded areas in the right side of the field with Tree Trunk Brown and a fairly dry sponge.

To balance out the field with the dominant color of lavender, dab in a few more flowers with the purple and white double-loaded sponge. Add a few more to the open field, but emphasize the purple flowers underneath the foreground tree.

waterfall

* Framed by colorful flowering trees, this thundering waterfall works its way over a sharp precipice and splashes into the river below. The mist from the falls softens the background colors and gives the feeling of great distance. In this mural project, you will learn just how to make water look transparent as it cascades over the boulders in the river and falls to the rocks below. You'll also see how to enliven trees and foliage with colors and highlights that reflect the light of the sun.

Color Mixes

1 Background Yellow
2 Tree Trunk Brown
3 Background Tree Green
4 Red Foliage
5 Lilac Accent
6 Gray Sky
7 Rock Undercolor
8 Brown Rock
9 Rock Highlight
10 Cool Gray
11 Titanium White
12 Dark Tree Green
13 Medium Tree Green
14 Highlight Green
15 Yellow Fall Leaves
16 Highlight Yellow
17 Dark Magenta
18 Medium Pink
19 Highlight Pink
20 Orange Leaves
21 Red-Orange

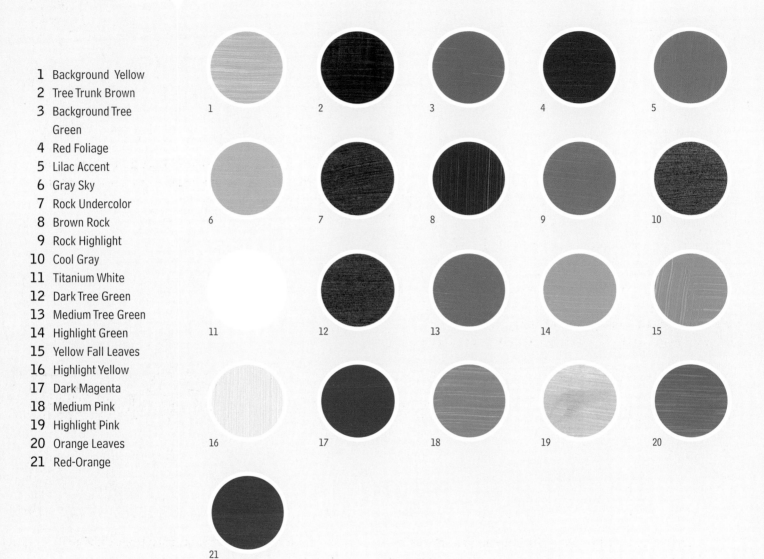

Background Trees

1 Lightly pencil in the top line of the waterfall, the main boulders, the trees on both sides of the falls, and the bottom of the falls. Using a spray bottle with clean water, lightly mist the surface to dampen. Load the sponge with Background Yellow and dab in the yellow tree leaves along the topmost edge of the painting.

2 Paint in the tree trunks and main branches with Tree Trunk Brown. Crunch the sponge and use the very edge of it to get these fine lines.

3 Using Background Tree Green, dab in green foliage along the line of background trees. Soften the edges and blend them into the yellow foliage color.

4 Accent several areas in the background trees with Red Foliage, but don't overdo it.

5 Dab in Lilac Accent under the trees to create flowering bushes in the background.

6 Load the sponge with thinned Gray Sky and wash this color over the trees and foliage to push them into the background and give them a misty look from the spray of the waterfall.

Rocks and Boulders

7 Load the sponge with Rock Undercolor. Use the top edge of the sponge and choppy horizontal motions to place in the rocks lining the banks at the top of the falls. Block in the larger boulders scattered in among the falling water and at the sides of the falls where they have fallen into rock piles. Go back in with more color to intensify and strengthen some of the rock faces.

8 With Brown Rock, begin shaping the faces and planes of the rocks using the flat face of the sponge. This warms up these rock faces where the sunlight strikes them. Skip the rocks at the very sides of the painting, as these will be covered up by the trees.

9 Add a bit of Titanium White to the Brown Rock color to get Rock Highlight. Load a corner of the sponge and highlight small areas of the rocks and boulders along the tops where they reflect light.

Waterfall

10 Thin Cool Gray with water to make a transparent wash. Begin the waterfall with horizontal streaks in the water above the falls. Deepen this color where the water comes up against the rocks along the bank and in the river. Using the top edge of a somewhat dry sponge, streak thinned Cool Gray vertically to form the face of the falls.

11 Continue making vertical streaks, allowing the white of the canvas to show through. Define the edge of the precipice by placing your sponge carefully at the beginning of each vertical stroke before pulling downward.

12 With Titanium White on a clean sponge, go over the Cool Gray undercolor. Use horizontal motions of the sponge in the river above the falls, and pull vertical streaks of white starting at the precipice and pulling downward, making sure you stay on the edge of the sponge. Pull white over parts of the rocks in the river to show water cascading over them.

13 With Titanium White on the sponge, layer more white streaks in the more turbulent areas of the waterfall where it hits the rocks and splashes into the water below. Make sure your streaks are vertical; water always falls in a straight line if unimpeded by other objects. Highlight the waves at the bottom of the falls, as well as the splash areas, with thicker white. Use the edge of your sponge to create little rivulets here and there along the boulders at the bottom of the falls.

Flowering Trees

14 For the trees on both sides of the waterfall, load a natural sea sponge with Dark Tree Green and dab on the first layer of foliage, leaving open spaces for the rocks to show through.

15 Dab on Medium Tree Green for the next lighter layer of leaves, allowing the darker leaves to show through.

16 Dab on Highlight Green here and there for the lightest layer of leaves where the sunlight hits them. Again, allow the first two layers of leaf color to show through.

17 Load the natural sea sponge with Yellow Fall Leaves and dab this color on the upper parts of the trees on both sides and up into the upper corners of the painting.

18 With Highlight Yellow, dab on the very lightest fall leaves here and there on the uppermost areas of the trees where the sunlight is brightest.

19 For the pinkish-purple flowering trees at the top left side of the falls, dab on the first layer of color with Dark Magenta on a natural sea sponge.

20 Dab on Medium Pink for the next layer of color, again using a natural sponge and allowing the darker pink undercolor to show through.

21 Use Highlight Pink on a natural sponge for the final layer on a few of the uppermost parts of the flowering trees where the light is brightest.

Foliage Color

22 Enrich the foliage colors by dabbing on Orange Leaves in a few areas of the trees, mostly on the right.

23 Deepen the foliage with some Red-Orange leaves in a very few areas.

24 Detail the trees with branches showing through here and there using Tree Trunk Brown on just the corner edge of a household sponge. Highlight the branches on only one side using the Rock Highlight color.

25 Add the final and brightest highlights to the trees with Titanium White dabbed on very sparingly.

26 With Medium Tree Green, stroke in some tall grass down at the bottom of the falls on both sides. Add reflections in the water under these foliage areas with the same green, making sure the reflections are directly underneath the foliage.

Critique

Step back from your work and take a critical look at all parts of your painting. Are there any areas that need a little bit more attention to detail? In this painting, the rocks along the upper riverbank are too dark and sharp-edged to look like background elements. Use the Gray Sky color from step 6 to soften and set back these rocks.

Add some yellow reflections in the water below the trees. Dry-sponge them on with the Yellow Fall Leaves color.

The trees need some dark leaves for contrast. Use Dark Tree Green and a natural sea sponge to reinstate some of the darker, shaded areas.

The finished mural is now balanced with warm, colorful foliage on three sides surrounding the cool grays and whites of the waterfall. Resist the temptation to overwork any type of falling water; the more paint you add, the more opaque the water becomes and the less realistic it looks.

edge of paradise

* Here is the stuff of dreams—a tropical paradise ablaze with the colors of the setting sun. Exotic flowers perfume the air, and a passing storm has refreshed the landscape. In this mural you will see how to paint the vivid hues of sunset, as well as dark storm clouds scudding low across the sky, a rocky island set in sharp relief against the last light of day, and the bright spark of color in the blooms of the bird of paradise.

Color Mixes

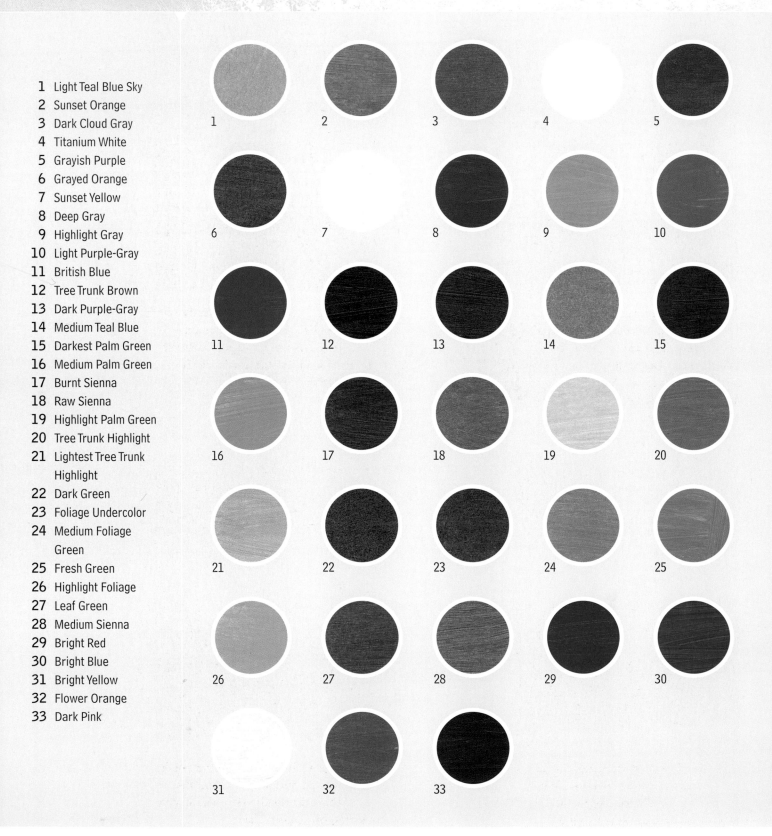

1 Light Teal Blue Sky
2 Sunset Orange
3 Dark Cloud Gray
4 Titanium White
5 Grayish Purple
6 Grayed Orange
7 Sunset Yellow
8 Deep Gray
9 Highlight Gray
10 Light Purple-Gray
11 British Blue
12 Tree Trunk Brown
13 Dark Purple-Gray
14 Medium Teal Blue
15 Darkest Palm Green
16 Medium Palm Green
17 Burnt Sienna
18 Raw Sienna
19 Highlight Palm Green
20 Tree Trunk Highlight
21 Lightest Tree Trunk
   Highlight
22 Dark Green
23 Foliage Undercolor
24 Medium Foliage
   Green
25 Fresh Green
26 Highlight Foliage
27 Leaf Green
28 Medium Sienna
29 Bright Red
30 Bright Blue
31 Bright Yellow
32 Flower Orange
33 Dark Pink

Sky, Water and Sunset

1   Lightly pencil in the horizon line and the placement of the center island, two palm trees and the foreground foliage. Use a spray bottle of clean water to lightly mist the surface. Wash in the sky area and background water with a thin layer of Light Teal Blue Sky.

2   Wash in Sunset Orange over the sky area just above the horizon where the sun is setting. Create the darker orange streaks with thicker paint and horizontal motions of the sponge.

3   Block in the storm clouds and the dark water area with Dark Cloud Gray. Sweep the sponge across the clouds to soften the edges and blend them into the sky color.

4   Lighten the tops of the storm clouds with puffy areas of Titanium White. Shape the clouds to look like they are scudding low across the bay.

Clouds and Distant Mountains

5 Add some Grayish Purple to the undersides of the clouds, and streak it into the orange sky color to show setting sun colors.

6 Load Grayed Orange onto the top edge of the sponge and draw in the far distant mountains along the horizon.

7 In the middle of the orange sky area, streak in some Sunset Yellow to indicate brighter sky where the sun has just set below the horizon. Lighten the top of the distant mountain with the same color.

8 Stroke in Deep Gray for the lower mountains in the distance just above the horizon.

Rocky Island

9 Block in the rocky island in the bay with Deep Gray, using the edge of the sponge to draw sharply defined edges. Dry-sponge the cast shadow on the water in front of the island. Highlight the lower gray mountains in the distance with Highlight Gray along the top edges.

10 Detail the island's craggy shapes with Light Purple-Gray on the areas that reflect light. Come back in with British Blue and highlight a few parts of the island.

11 Streak Dark Purple-Gray into the water to show reflections of the cloud colors. In the foreground water, deepen the color even more with thicker layers of this color. With Medium Teal Blue, deepen the color of the water on both sides of the island.

12 Blend the Medium Teal Blue forward into the darker foreground water, using horizontal strokes of the sponge. Dry-sponge Titanium White streaks in the water for highlights and reflections.

Palm Trees

13 Load the top edge of the sponge with Tree Trunk Brown. Draw in the palm tree trunks, widening the trunks at the top. Outline some of the palm frond stems with the same color.

14 With Darkest Palm Green, pull out the palm leaves from the stems; the shortest leaves are at the tip ends. Dry-sponging the palm leaves gives separation and shape to the palm fronds.

15 Dry-sponge some Medium Palm Green highlights onto the palm fronds.

16 Dry-sponge some Burnt Sienna in a few places to show dried-up, brown palm leaves. Highlight these areas with a little Raw Sienna. Highlight the green areas of the fronds with Highlight Palm Green. With Tree Trunk Highlight, highlight the front stems and the main tree trunks. Add a second highlight to the trunks with Lightest Tree Trunk Highlight. Detail the areas where the bases of the palm fronds attach to the trunks with these two highlight colors.

Foreground Foliage

17 Begin the foliage in the foreground by dabbing on Foliage Undercolor with a natural sea sponge.

18 Deepen the shadowed and low areas of the foliage with Dark Green.

19 Highlight the tops of the foliage with Medium Foliage Green.

20 Block in some areas of new growth with Fresh Green. Draw in some large leaves at left under the palm trees.

21 Dab on Highlight Foliage where the sunlight hits the leaves along the top edges.

22 Enrich the color of the large leaves under the palm trees with Leaf Green.

Bird of Paradise

23 With Dark Green, stroke in the shapes of the bird of paradise leaves and stems.

24 With Medium Foliage Green, use the edge of the sponge to place the central vein line, then pull short straight strokes inward toward the vein line to create the ruffled surface of each leaf.

25 Highlight the leaf ruffles with Highlight Foliage.

26 Wash some Leaf Green along the central veins to deepen and shade them.

27 Touch Medium Sienna here and there on the leaves and underneath in the foliage area.

28 With Dark Green, draw in the flower pod and stem on the bird of paradise.

 29 Highlight the flower pod with Fresh Green.

 30 Begin the crown with short strokes of Titanium White.

31 Add petals to the crown with strokes of Bright Red.

 32 Add two central petals of Bright Blue.

33 Under-highlight the red petals with Bright Yellow.

Tropical Flowers

34 In the foliage area underneath the palm trees, add bright spots of flower colors starting with Flower Orange.

35 The next flowers are dabbed in with Dark Pink.

36 While the Dark Pink flowers are still wet, lighten and highlight them with Titanium White on the corner of the sponge.

37 With Medium Foliage Green, dab in foliage that covers the base of the bird of paradise and overlaps the flower area under the palm trees. This will set some of the flowers back into the shade.

Critique

Step back from your work and take a critical look at all parts of your painting. Are there any areas that need a little bit more attention to detail? Are the colors balanced and harmonious? In this painting, some of the bird of paradise leaves need to be reinstated with Darkest Palm Green. Also, the palm fronds on the tall trees need some deeper shading with the same color. The storm clouds need just a bit more darkening in the lower areas with Grayish Purple.

red roses

* Murals of landscapes or scenery are sometimes just too large and overwhelming if you have a small space you wish to decorate. Try painting a still life to suit the size and space available, such as this one of roses in a cut glass vase on a dark tabletop. In this painting, you'll learn how to glaze background colors until they are deep, rich and textured. You'll also find an easy way to paint clear glass with just a few well-placed strokes of the sponge. Finally, you'll see how easy it is to paint roses of many colors—no need to stroke on one petal at a time.

Color Mixes

1 Raw Sienna
2 Burnt Sienna
3 Yellow Ochre
4 Burnt Umber
5 Titanium White
6 Dark Green
7 Yellow-Green
8 Lightest Green
9 Yellow Leaves
10 Darkest Rose
11 Dark Rose
12 Dark Pink
13 Deep Orange
14 Bud Red
15 Bright Red
16 Deep Pink
17 Medium Orange
18 Medium Pink
19 Highlight Pink

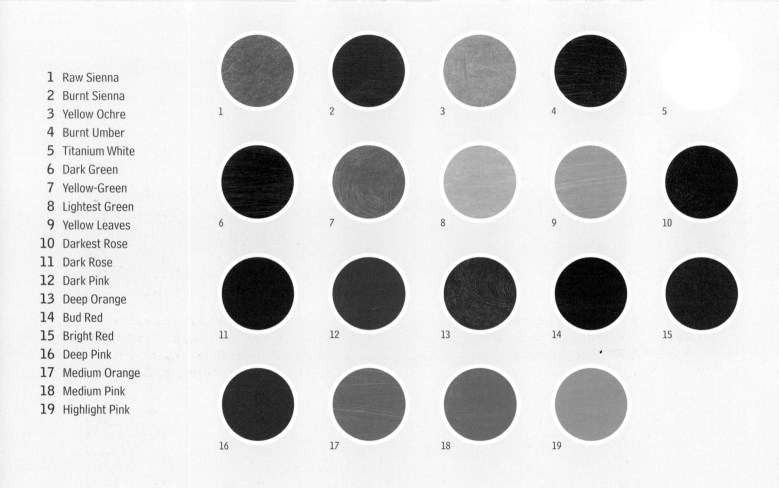

Glazed Background

1 Lightly pencil in the line of the table and the placement of the glass vase, the rose blossoms and leaves. Use a spray bottle of clean water to lightly mist the surface. Wash in the entire background with Raw Sienna.

2 While the Raw Sienna wash is still wet, load the sponge with Burnt Sienna and glaze the outer areas surrounding the center. Do not smooth it out or overwork the glaze—let it retain a slightly mottled texture.

3 Load the sponge with Yellow Ochre and glaze the center area behind where the roses will be. Blend it out into the Burnt Sienna glaze so there are no hard edges.

4 Wash in the final background glaze around the left side and along the bottom with Burnt Umber that has been darkened with a little black. With a thicker glaze, indicate the top of the table the vase sits on, using the edge of the sponge and following the pencil line.

Glass Vase and Leaves

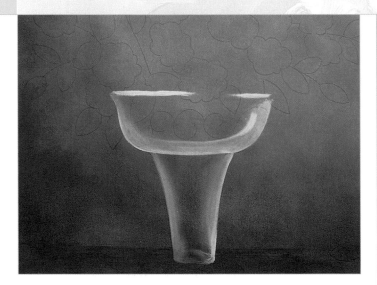

5 The glass vase is painted with Titanium White. Sketch in the outside edges using the very edge of the sponge. Turn the sponge over to the clean side and lay the edge on the white line. Pull the white inward to indicate roundness, gradating and softening the white until it fades out completely.

6 With Dark Green, use the edge of the sponge to indicate the stems in the vase and the darkest leaves under the rose bouquet. Extend a few stems outward. Use the corner of the sponge to shape the leaves and draw vein lines.

7 With Yellow-Green, block in some lighter green leaves and highlight one side of the stems in the vase. Shape the outside edge of the leaves and add vein lines.

8 Load the edge of the sponge with Lightest Green and draw in the lightest leaves. With the Yellow Leaves color, add a few subtle yellow leaves in the background.

Rose Shapes

9 Start the roses by indicating their basic shapes with thick paint. Begin with Darkest Rose color.

10 Working from the darkest colors to the lightest, the next roses are painted with Dark Rose color.

11 Next, block in the Dark Pink rose shapes.

12 For interest, add a couple of Deep Orange rose shapes.

13 Finish blocking in the bouquet by adding four small rosebuds on the stem extending outward. Use Bud Red on the corner of the sponge for these.

Rose Petals

14 With Bright Red on the edge of your sponge, stroke in petals on the Darkest Rose shapes. If the base color has already dried, reinstate it before adding the petal color.

15 With Deep Pink on the edge of your sponge, stroke in petals on the Dark Rose shapes.

16 With Medium Orange, stroke in petals on the Deep Orange shapes. Place Medium Pink petals on the Dark Pink rose shapes.

17 Highlight some of the outer petals on most of the roses with small touches of Highlight Pink.

18 To finish the painting, go back in with Titanium White and add detail to the glass vase. First, reinstate the top edge of the vase under the lower leaves and roses. Then draw a design on the bowl using the edge and corner of the sponge and following the pencil lines. To show reflections in the lower part of the vase, streak upward with white, fading off as you approach the area shaded by the bowl.

Critique

Step back and take a critical look at your painting. Are there areas that need more detailing? Are the colors balanced and harmonious? In this painting, the glass vase is casting a reflection on the tabletop; draw that in with Titanium White. Place some fallen leaves on the table underneath the bouquet with Dark Green, and add a few leaves in the bouquet that overlap the roses and set them back.

The tabletop needs still more interest, so highlight the dark green leaves with Yellow-Green. Add a few fallen rose petals with Darkest Rose highlighted with Titanium White.

The tabletop needs to be darker to give it some weight and help ground the vase of flowers. Come back in with the Burnt Umber glaze and deepen the tabletop and along the sides. Add cast shadows under the fallen leaves and petals. Highlight the lightest green leaves with small touches of white.

15 Murals in 3 Easy Steps

*

In Part One, we learned how to use sponge-painting techniques to achieve many different elements commonly found in mural designs for the home. These elements include skies, clouds, water, trees, grasses, flowers, mountains, waterfalls, landscapes, and much more.

In Part Two, we present fifteen new murals to try. Each of these murals uses one or more of the elements you learned about in the six murals presented earlier. We have combined these elements into interesting new designs so you will see how the same technique can produce many different effects.

Each of these fifteen murals is broken down into three steps. You will see how each design is pulled together using elements you have already learned how to paint. If you are unsure about a certain technique, just refer back to one of the six fully demonstrated murals in Part One.

The first section, titled "Beaches and Coastlines," includes four new murals that feature sandy beaches, palm trees, rocky cliffs, ocean waves, blue skies, puffy white clouds and more.

The second section is called "Landscapes" and here you'll find five new murals with such elements as quiet country roads, flowering shrubs, trees and foliage in all colors.

The three new murals in the third section, "Rivers and Waterfalls," include calm and reflective water, rocks and boulders, and riverbanks lined with colorful foliage.

Finally, "Floral Still Lifes" features three new murals with ideas for painting a variety of flowers in interesting containers, such as a copper bowl and a decorative bronze urn.

Color Tips

The colors used in all the following step-by-step demonstrations are mixes made with waterbased acrylic paints. You can find hundreds of acrylic colors in convenient 2-oz. (57g) bottles at your local craft supply store. The color charts at the beginning of each demonstration are meant to help you match the colors you buy as closely as possible to the colors used in painting each mural. With so many colors available, you should have no trouble finding the ones you need. If you prefer, you can make your own color palette to suit your home, or change the colors used in these murals to ones you like better.

"Palm Heights"

Beaches and Coastlines

Yellow Skies

Color Mixes

1 Light Sky Yellow
2 Golden Yellow
3 Sea Green
4 Sand Brown
5 Gray-Purple
6 Purple-Gray
7 Titanium White
8 Seafoam Green
9 Olive Green
10 Raw Sienna
11 Light Olive
12 Sea Oats Brown
13 Sea Grapes Green
14 Highlight Green
15 Sage Green
16 Dark Red

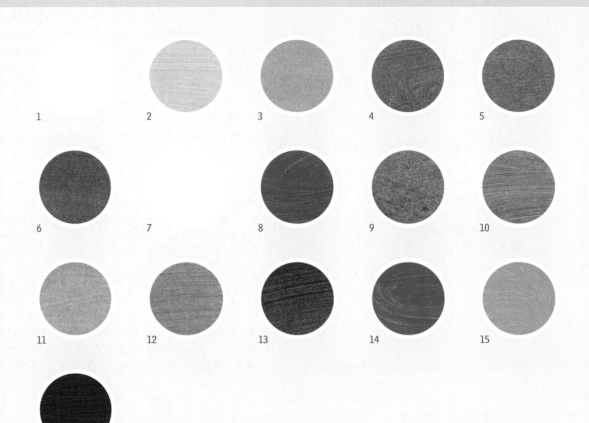

1 Wash in the sky and water areas with Light Sky Yellow. Deepen the upper sky area with a Golden Yellow wash. Wash in the seawater with Sea Green. Wash in the sandy beach area with a light layer of thinned Sand Brown, then come back in with thicker Sand Brown and mottle in some shadowed areas. Streak a little Golden Yellow into the seawater to show the reflection from the sky.

2 Map the clouds with Gray-Purple, blocking them in at the sides and streaking color out into the center. Deepen the undersides with Purple-Gray. Streak this same color lightly into the seawater, and shade the low places in the sand. Lighten areas in the clouds with Titanium White, and create low waves rolling into shore with the same white. Brighten the high places in the sandy beach with thinned white, using thicker white for highlights. In the seawater, indicate deeper water with Seafoam Green. Shade the undersides of rolling waves with Purple-Gray to create contrast with the white tops.

3 Indicate low grasses in the sand with short upward strokes of Olive Green and Raw Sienna, highlighted with Light Olive. Stroke in the sea oats on the right side with Sea Oats Brown, then highlight with Olive Green. With Sea Grapes Green, stroke in the stems of the sea grapes shrub and dab on the rounded leaves, thicker nearer the base and sparser nearer the top. Highlight with Highlight Green, and add some lighter Sage Green leaves and Raw Sienna leaves. The flowers are Dark Red, highlighted with Titanium White. Shade underneath the grasses and under the sea grapes shrub with Purple-Gray.

Palm Heights

Color Mixes

1 Dusk Purple	7 Bright Yellow	12 Dark Blue
2 Dusk Pink	8 Rust	13 Raw Sienna
3 Light Yellow	9 Dark Brown	14 Burnt Sienna
4 Orange	10 Dark Palm Green	15 Dark Teal Blue
5 Bright Red	11 Medium Palm	
6 Titanium White	Green	

1

2

3

4

5

6

7

8

9

10

11

12

13

14

15

1 Using a spray bottle of clean water, lightly mist the surface to dampen. Wash in the sky undercolor with Dusk Purple at the top and Dusk Pink over the rest of the surface. Mottle in sunset-lit clouds with areas of Light Yellow, Orange, Bright Red and Titanium White.

2 Intensify the clouds with more Bright Red in a few areas, some Titanium White to brighten the lightest clouds in the upper sky, and Bright Yellow and Rust for the clouds nearest the horizon where the setting sun is throwing the warmest light on them.

3 Stroke in the palm tree trunks with Dark Brown. The palm fronds are blocked in with Dark Palm Green and the leaves pulled out with a dry sponge. The leaves are highlighted with Medium Palm Green, then touches of Bright Red are applied as reflections of the sunset colors. Apply Dark Blue in the inner areas to shade where the palm fronds attach to the trunk. Accent here and there with Raw Sienna. Shape and highlight the tree trunks with Burnt Sienna, and shade down one side of each tree trunk with Dark Teal Blue. Use Bright Red to highlight the sunlit areas of the tree trunks.

Coastal Cliffs

Color Mixes

1 Gray-Blue
2 Dark Gray-Blue
3 Dark Rock Gray
4 Medium Brown
5 Red Sienna
6 Greenish Blue
7 Titanium White
8 Gray-Purple
9 Bright Blue
10 Taupe
11 Raw Sienna
12 Dark Brown
13 Dark Foliage Green
14 Medium Foliage Green
15 Cool Brown

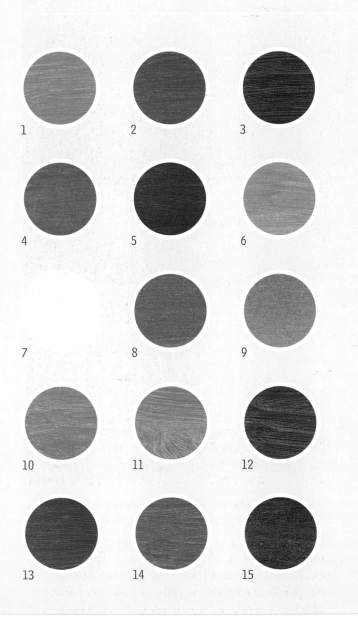

1 Using a spray bottle of clean water, lightly mist the surface to dampen. Wash Gray-Blue over the sky and ocean areas. Darken the top of the sky with Dark Gray-Blue and streak some of this color into the water. With Dark Rock Gray, block in the rocks of the cliff. Loosely wash in highlights with Medium Brown. With Red Sienna, add a mid-value color to the rocks. Wash over all the water and sky area with Greenish Blue.

2 Add clouds in the sky area with Titanium White. Paint puffy clouds at the top, and streak in some flatter clouds at the horizon. The waves are painted in with Titanium White, and the further back they go, the more their edges are softened and blended into the water. Enhance the water with Gray-Purple to show shadows and low places, and Bright Blue for sky reflections.

3 Finish the rocks by shaping their sides first with Taupe, then highlight with Titanium White. With Raw Sienna, add some brighter, warmer spots on the rocks, and shade some of the sides with Burnt Sienna. Begin the Monterey pine trees with trunks and branches of Dark Brown. The first layer of foliage is Dark Foliage Green. Highlight the topmost areas with Medium Foliage Green. Shade underneath the foliage and along the trunks with Cool Brown.

Palm Dunes

Color Mixes

1 Green-Blue	7 Burnt Sienna	13 Dark Cream
2 Sky Blue	8 Payne's Gray	14 Grass Green
3 Cream	9 Medium Brown	15 Light Yellow-Green
4 Dark Sand Brown	10 Light Brown	16 Yellow Ochre
5 Titanium White	11 Dark Palm Green	17 Dark Pink
6 Raw Sienna	12 Medium Green	18 Violet

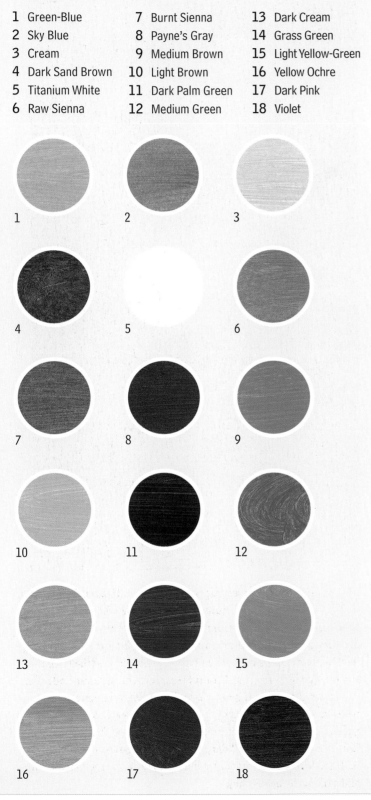

1 Using a spray bottle of clean water, lightly mist the surface to dampen. Wash Green-Blue over the sky, leaving some areas unpainted for clouds. Intensify parts of the sky with Sky Blue. Wash in the sand dunes with Cream. Add dips and shadows and indicate some dried foliage with Dark Sand Brown.

2 Add very soft clouds in the sky with Titanium White. Use Raw Sienna to warm some areas of the sand, and Burnt Sienna where there are heavy dips and low places. Highlight the high areas of the sand with Titanium White, and intensify the shadowed sides of the sand dunes with Payne's Gray. Dry-sponge some thinned Payne's Gray in the low path area and in some of the shadowed areas of the sand.

3 Begin the palm tree trunks with Dark Sand Brown. Highlight with Medium Brown, then highlight again with Light Brown. Stroke in the palm frond stems with Dark Palm Green, then dry-sponge thc leaves outward from the stems. Highlight the fronds with Medium Green, then dab in Burnt Sienna here and there. The lightest highlights are Dark Cream. Stroke some grassy areas under the palm trees and in the sand with Grass Green. Stroke in darker grasses wtih Dark Palm Green. Highlight with Light Yellow-Green. Add dried grasses with Cream, and warm up the grassy areas with Yellow Ochre. Dab in some flowers with Yellow Ochre plus Titanium White, Dark Pink and Violet. Shade underneath the grasses and strengthen the edge of the hill with Payne's Gray.

Landscapes

Wintry Yellow

Color Mixes

1 Cool Gray
2 Warm Gray
3 Naples Yellow
4 Raw Sienna
5 Shadow Brown
6 Blue-Gray
7 Background Tree Brown
8 Highlight Brown
9 Very Dark Brown
10 Medium Highlight Brown
11 Burnt Sienna
12 Dark Green
13 Highlight Green
14 Red Leaf
15 Bright Red
16 Orange-Red

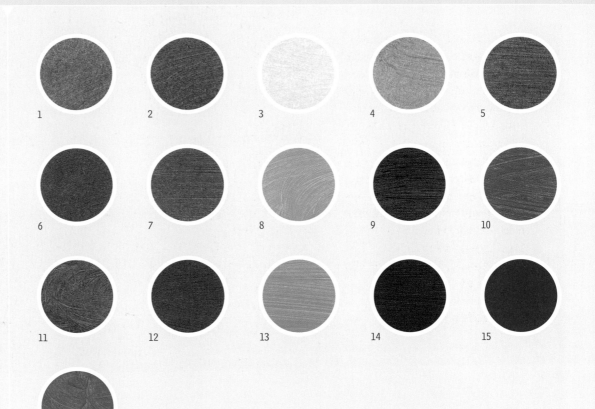

1 Dab and drag a household sponge loaded with Cool Gray along the top area to indicate background trees. With Warm Gray, loosely draw some individual tree shapes in the background. Wash over the rest of the area below the tree line with Naples Yellow. Warm up the lower and top areas with Raw Sienna, and set in some shading with Shadow Brown where the foreground trees will be.

2 Shade very subtly under the background trees with Blue-Gray. Shade the most distant areas of the field with Warm Gray, and intensify with Shadow Brown. Warm some areas with thinned Raw Sienna, especially in the foreground. The bare trees in the background are stroked in with an undercolor of Background Tree Brown, then highlighted with Highlight Brown. The larger foreground trees are stroked in with Very Dark Brown undercolor, as are the shadows and dark foliage under the trees. The bark of these trees is detailed with Medium Highlight Brown and Burnt Sienna.

3 Dab in some Dark Green for foliage under the large foreground trees and tip with Highlight Green. Add streaks of tall grass in the foreground with Naples Yellow. Shade under the shrub with Very Dark Brown. Draw in the branches with an undercolor of Very Dark Brown and highlight with Highlight Brown. Dab on some sparse foliage with Dark Green and highlight here and there with Highlight Green, maintaining open spaces on the branches. Dot some Red Leaf color on the shrub, then a little Bright Red, and finally a little Orange-Red. Use the same colors for the fallen leaves underneath the shrub.

Morning Glow

Color Mixes

1 Warm Gray
2 Titanium White
3 Light Brown
4 Burnt Sienna
5 Raw Umber
6 Dark Olive
7 Undercolor Green
8 Darkest Green
9 Blue Sky
10 Warm Cream
11 Medium Green
12 Highlight Green
13 Blue-Green
14 Dried Leaves
   Orange
15 Dark Brown
16 Medium Brown
17 Terra Cotta
18 Fleshtone
19 Bright Purple
20 Bright Blue
21 Bright Red
22 Burgundy
23 Yellow Ochre
24 Palest Green

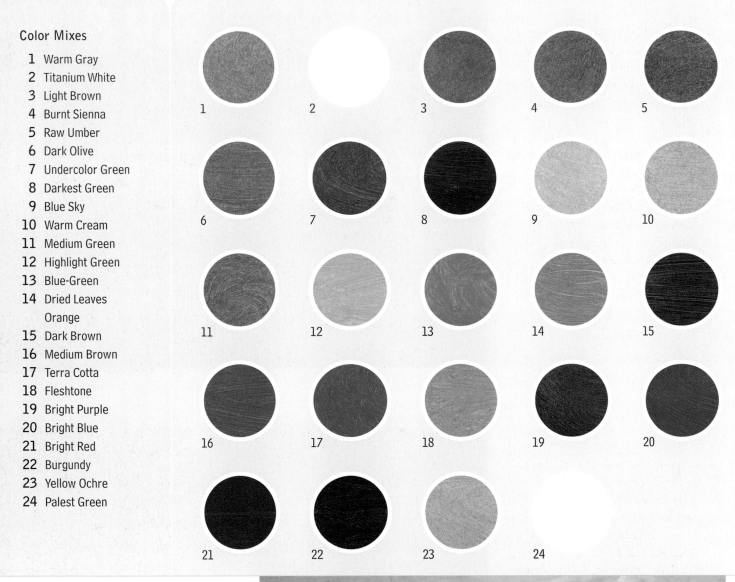

1 Wash in the sky area with Warm Gray and indicate clouds with Titanium White. Block in the background trees and shrubs with Light Brown, the path with Burnt Sienna and Raw Umber, and the foliage with Dark Olive, Undercolor Green and Darkest Green.

2 Enhance the sky color with Blue Sky and strengthen some of the clouds with Titanium White. Glaze the lower sky area with Warm Cream to show the glow of sunrise. Streak some low white clouds just above the horizon. Set the distant part of the path into the background with Warm Gray, and bring the foreground path forward with white. With a natural sponge and Darkest Green, extend some of the foliage out onto the path. Lighten a few areas with Medium Green, then Highlight Green. Enrich the foliage with Blue-Green and indicate dried leaves with Dried Leaves Orange.

3 Draw in the trunks and branches of the midground trees with Dark Brown, then shape with Medium Brown. With a natural sponge and Terra Cotta, dab in the tree leaves, then highlight with Fleshtone. Sponge in distant flowers with Bright Purple and Bright Blue, then dot in a few Bright Purple flowers highlighted with white in the left foreground. Dot in colorful flowers in the foliage areas with Bright Red, Burgundy, and Yellow Ochre, highlighting all with Titanium White. Come back in with Darkest Green and strengthen the shadows in the foliage along the pathway. With Highlight Green paint some grasses overlapping the flowers, and add final highlights with Palest Green.

Golden Banks

Color Mixes

1 Dusty Pink
2 Gray-Blue
3 Gray-Purple
4 Titanium White
5 Yellow Ochre
6 Olive Green
7 Medium Green
8 Aqua Blue
9 Foliage Red
10 Raw Sienna
11 Brown-Violet
12 Yellow-Green
13 Highlight Green
14 Bright Green
15 Tree Trunk Brown
16 Mid-Brown
17 Burnt Sienna
18 Dark Tree Green
19 Foliage Green
20 Purple Blossom
21 Red Blossom
22 Blue Blossom

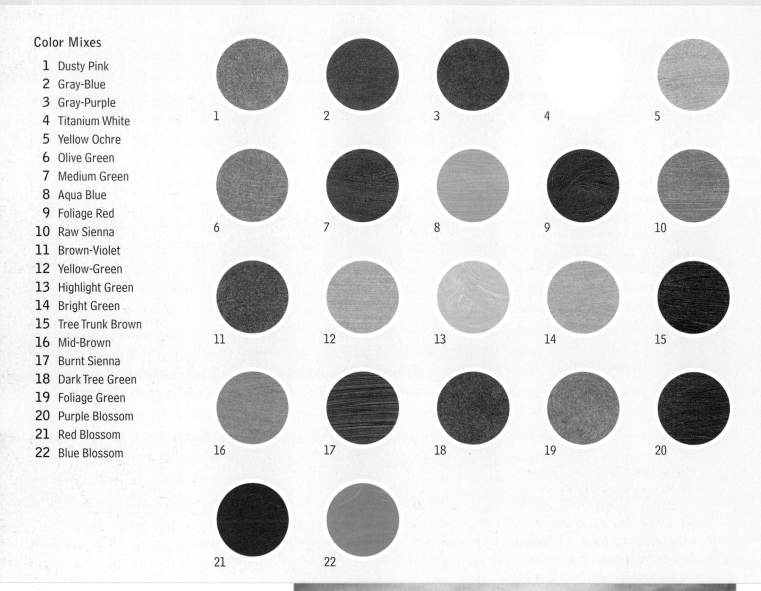

1 Wash in the sky area with Dusty Pink. Use Gray-Blue for the upper left corner, and Gray-Purple for the upper right. Shape the clouds with Titanium White. Block in the riverbanks with Yellow Ochre and the foreground grass with Olive Green shaded with Medium Green. Wash in the river with horizontal strokes of thinned Gray-Blue.

2 With Aqua Blue, Foliage Red and Yellow Ochre, indicate the far distant trees; use the same colors to suggest reflections in the water. Intensify the land area on both sides of the river with Raw Sienna. Use Brown-Violet to delineate the riverbanks and to indicate the shadows cast on the water by the riverbanks. Streak Titanium White into the water to show movement and flow. In the foreground grass area, add strokes of Yellow-Green grasses and highlight here and there with Highlight Green and Bright Green.

3 Draw in the tree trunks and branches with Tree Trunk Brown, then use Mid-Brown to highlight and give them a rounded shape. Accent with Burnt Sienna and Titanium White. Use a natural sponge and Dark Tree Green to apply the foliage undercolor, then add Highlight Green. Dab on Yellow Ochre foliage mostly on the right-hand tree, then highlight again with Highlight Green to show sunlit leaves. Working wet-into-wet, dab blossoms into and underneath the trees as follows: Purple Blossom for the left tree, Blue Blossom for the middle tree, and Red Blossom for the right tree. All are highlighted with Titanium White. Set back and overlap the tree foliage, grass and blossoms with Bright Green.

Soft Vibrance

Color Mixes

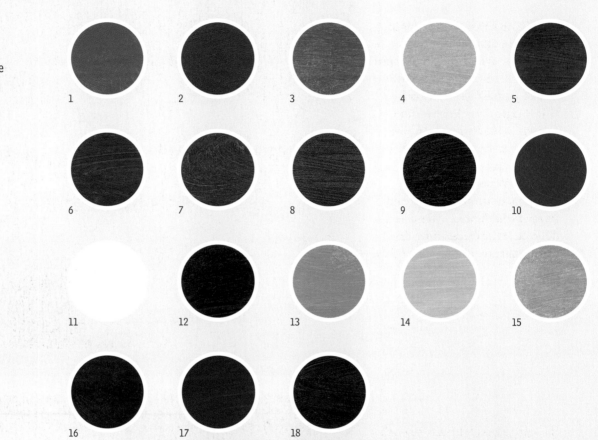

1 Dusky Purple
2 Distant Tree Purple
3 Foreground Green
4 Yellow-Green
5 Water Blue
6 Burnt Sienna
7 Red Clay
8 Deep Magenta
9 Dirt Brown
10 Scarlet
11 Titanium White
12 Dark Teal
13 Grass Green
14 Highlight Green
15 Yellow Ochre
16 Shadow Green
17 Magenta
18 Bright Purple

1 Wash in the sky color with Dusky Purple. Sponge in the far distant trees with Distant Tree Purple. Block in the foreground foliage with Foregound Green and the middle-ground foliage with Yellow-Green. Block in the creek with Water Blue. The dirt road is mottled in with Burnt Sienna.

2 With Distant Tree Purple, draw in the two trees at left and dab on foliage sparingly, leaving lots of open spaces. Intensify the dirt road with Red Clay, and shade the edges with Deep Magenta. Darken a few areas of the road in the distance with Dirt Brown, and enrich the foreground road with Scarlet. With thinned Titanium White, haze over the background sky area to soften and set it into the distance. Haze over the dirt road and the trees with a dry sponge and thinned Titanium White.

3 Shade the edges of the curving creek with Dark Teal. Stroke in tall grasses and reeds along the creek and make a few reflections in the water with Grass Green, then highlight a few areas with Highlight Green. Dab some Yellow Ochre into the grasses, then indicate low places and shadows with Shadow Green. Highlight here and there with Grass Green. The flowers on both sides of the creek are Magenta and Water Blue, highlighted with Titanium White. Dab in some Bright Purple flowers in the same areas and again highlight with white. Finish with some tall grasses of Yellow-Green overlapping the flowers.

Color Mixes

 1 Gray-Blue
 2 Gray-Green
 3 Raw Umber
 4 Dark Green
 5 Yellow Grass
 6 Olive Green
 7 Grass Green
 8 Light Brown
 9 Burnt Sienna
10 Titanium White
11 Tree Green
12 Highlight Green
13 Lightest Green
14 Dirt Brown
15 Cream
16 Dried Bushes
17 Red Clay
18 Light Red Clay
19 Medium Blue
20 Dark Blue
21 Light Blue
22 Purple-Blue
23 Red
24 Light Pink
25 Violet
26 Magenta
27 Golden-Yellow

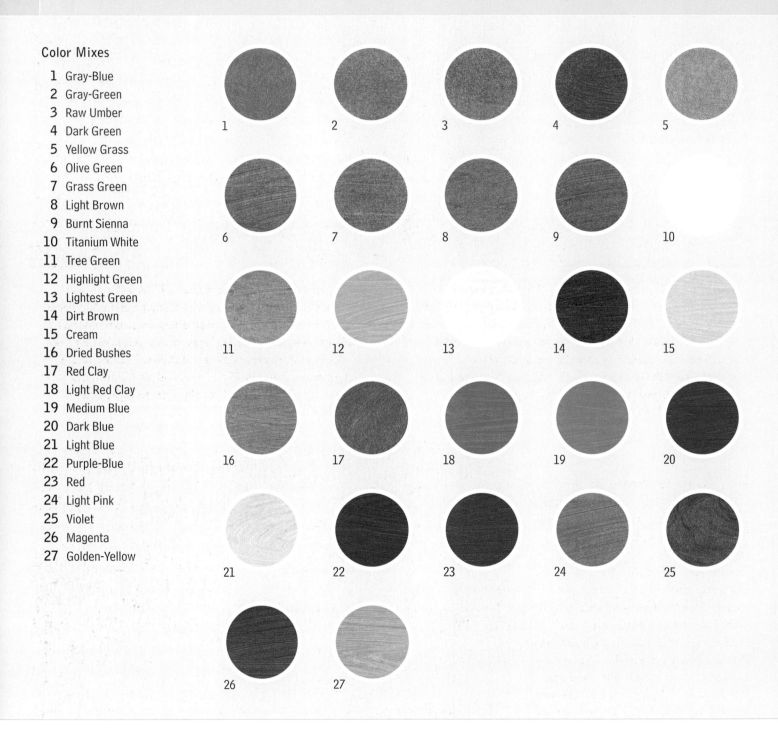

1 Wash in the sky with Gray-Blue. Block in the distant mountains and hills with Gray-Green, and indicate trees on the hillsides with Raw Umber. Begin the midground trees with Dark Green undercolor. The foreground foliage is blocked in with areas of Yellow Grass and Olive Green on the left side, shaded with Dark Green. On the right side of the road, wash in Grass Green and shade with Dark Green. Wash in the dirt road with Light Brown, mottled with Burnt Sienna.

2 Highlight the far distant mountains with Yellow-Green, and enhance with Olive Green and a bit of Burnt Sienna. Add clouds of Titanium White and soften the distant mountaintops to look like low-hanging clouds. Highlight the evergreens near the road with Tree Green, then with Highlight Green. The trees on the right are enriched with Olive Green. With Dirt Brown, shade the road's edges and low places. Highlight the high places with Cream.

3 With a natural sponge, dab in Highlight Green for the lightest foliage on both sides of the road. Extend this into the road in a few places to soften the edges. The dried bushes on the right are Red Clay highlighted with Light Red Clay. For the blue flowers on the left, the undercolor is Medium Blue, the shading is Dark Blue, and the highlight is Light Blue. Add sparks of Purple-Blue here and there in the blue flowers. On the right side of the road, the Red flowers are highlighted with Light Pink, and the tall Violet flowers are highlighted with white wet-into-wet. The Golden-Yellow flowers are also highlighted with white. On the left, the Magenta flowers are highlighted wet-into-wet with white. Use Lightest Green and a natural sponge to dab in the lightest flowers on both sides to overlap and set back the others.

Rivers and Waterfalls

Reflections

Color Mixes

1. Burnt Sienna
2. Camel Brown
3. Muted Blue
4. Cool Gray
5. Dark Aquamarine
6. Light Olive
7. Dark Olive
8. Thalo Blue
9. Peachy Cream
10. Lavender
11. Bright Yellow
12. Powder Blue
13. Periwinkle
14. Soft Pink
15. Light Sage
16. Thalo Green
17. Gray-Brown
18. Light Gray-Brown
19. Distant Green
20. Grayed Yellow-Green
21. Light Green
22. Light Yellow-Green
23. Magenta
24. Titanium White

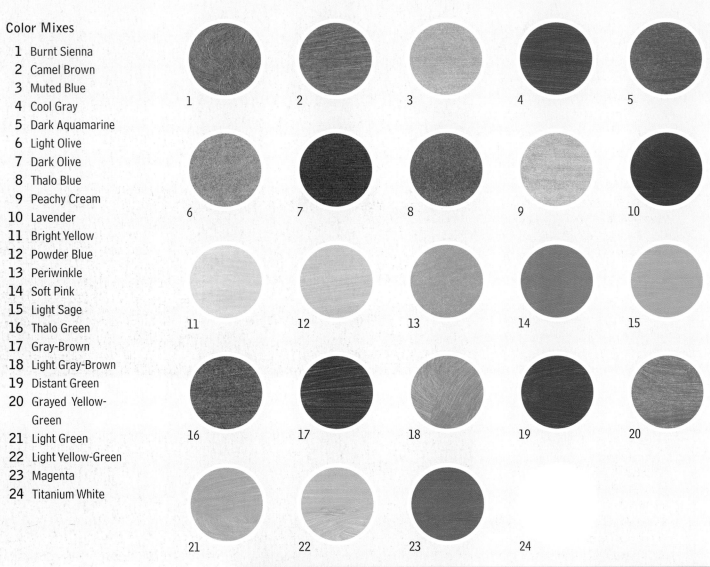

1. Use a natural sponge and Burnt Sienna and Camel Brown to dab on the background trees and foliage. With a household sponge, wash over the sky and water areas with Muted Blue. Use Cool Gray to suggest background trees on both sides. The distant bushes are Dark Aquamarine. Wash in the landmass with Light Olive, and place shadows and grassy areas with Dark Olive. Block in the edges of the water with Thalo Blue, avoiding the center. Blend Peachy Cream into the center sky area, and into the center of the water to create a reflection.

2 Dab in some distant drifts of flowers, first with Lavender, then with Bright Yellow, then Thalo Blue, Powder Blue, Periwinkle, and Soft Pink. Use these same colors for the foreground flowers. Dry-sponge grass throughout the foreground with Light Sage. Mist the water area with clean water. With Thalo Green, create shadows on the water and shade the edges of the landmass. Go over this color with Thalo Blue to deepen the shadows. Sweep highlights on the water with Powder Blue to show motion and flow.

3 Stroke on all the tree trunks and branches with Gray-Brown and highlight with Light Gray-Brown. With Distant Green, dab on the first layer of tree leaves and shade the ground underneath the trees. Highlight the leaves on the trees with Grayed Yellow-Green; highlight again with Light Green, then again with Light Yellow-Green. On the foreground tree, dab on some blossoms with Soft Pink. Use Thalo Green to place lily pads along the edges of the water. Top the lily pads with Magenta flowers highlighted with Titanium White. Indicate a few reflections in the water with tiny streaks of thinned white.

Paradise Fall

Color Mixes

1 Sky Blue	8 Dark Palm Green	15 Foliage Green
2 Deep Blue	9 Violet-Gray	16 Fern Green
3 Titanium White	10 Dusky Pink	17 Fern Highlight
4 Cream	11 Deep Gold	18 Highlight Brown
5 Reddish-Brown	12 Rust	19 Dark Red
6 Burnt Sienna	13 Dark Violet	
7 Dark Brown	14 Payne's Gray	

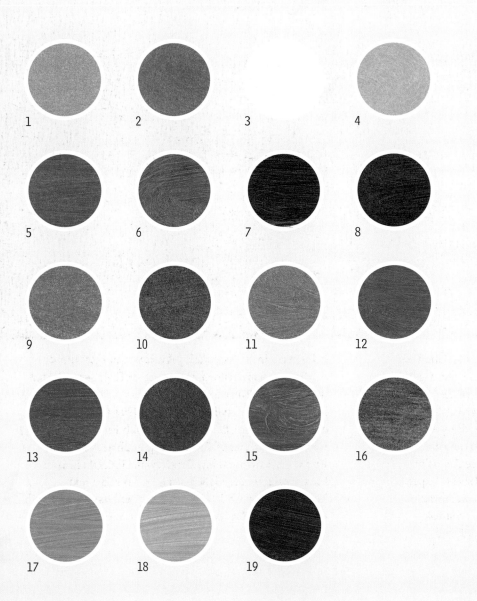

1 Wash in the entire sky area and the river with Sky Blue, then deepen the upper sky with Deep Blue. Block in the clouds with Titanium White. The far distant mountain in the middle is blocked in with Cream and shaped with Reddish-Brown. Use Burnt Sienna to block in the two side mountains and the cliff face. Shape and shade them with Dark Brown. The large palm leaves are blocked in with Dark Palm Green. Use Violet-Gray to vertically streak in the undercolor for the waterfall.

2 Shade the clouds with Dusky Pink in some areas and Deep Gold and Rust in others. With Titanium White, strengthen the denser cloud masses. Highlight the tops of the mountains with thinned Sky Blue and the upward facing rocks with Cream. Dab in Dark Palm Green foliage on the left side. Deepen the river water with Deep Blue, then with Dark Violet to show waves. Streak Deep Blue down the waterfall in places. Shade the cliff sides and rocky shapes with Payne's Gray. With Titanium White, streak turbulent water in the river; emphasize the precipice and streak downward on the falls; add rivulets on the cliff and splashing water at the bottom.

3 Paint stems in the large dark palm leaves, and dry-sponge the leaves to show ruffled texture with Foliage Green. Enrich the leaves with Burnt Sienna in a few places. The ferns are stroked in with an undercolor of Fern Green using the very edge of the sponge, then highlighted with Fern Highlight color. The branches of the flowering shrub are stroked in with Dark Brown and highlighted with Highlight Brown. Place blossoms of Dark Red along the branches, and highlight them with Titanium White. Paint the spiky leaves with Dark Palm Green highlighted with Foliage Green.

River Path

Color Mixes

1 Sky Blue	7 Thalo Green	12 Yellow-Green
2 Deep Green	8 Light Golden	13 Emerald
3 Water Blue	Yellow	14 Dark Blue
4 Cream	9 Terra Cotta	15 Titanium White
5 Burnt Sienna	10 Highlight Brown	
6 Dark Brown	11 Mid-Gray	

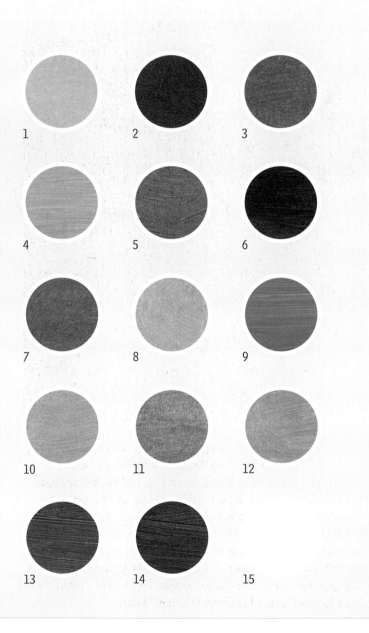

1 Wash in the sky with Sky Blue. With Deep Green on a natural sponge, dab in the dark background foliage. The river water is dabbed in with Water Blue to indicate little waves. Block in and shape the rocks and boulders with Cream for the tops, Burnt Sienna for the midtones, and Dark Brown for the undersides and shading. The river sand is Cream mottled with Burnt Sienna to indicate dips and low spots. The airy-looking foliage in the background is lightly dabbed on with Thalo Green on a natural sponge.

2 Stroke on the trees in the far background with Burnt Sienna and Terra Cotta. The closer trees are Dark Brown, shaped with Burnt Sienna and Highlight Brown. Set back the trees with overlapping Light Golden Yellow foliage. Shade the trees and foliage with Deep Green. Finish the background rocks with Cream on the top sides. Dab some Mid-Gray into the foreground rocks to shade.

3 Deepen the shadows in the background foliage with Emerald and Thalo Green. Wash thinned Yellow-Green over the background water. Stroke Water Blue and Dark Blue in the midground water, Emerald in the calmer foreground water, and Dark Brown in the shallows. Deepen the shadows around the river boulders with Dark Blue. With Titanium White, dab in the water cascading over the rocks, the water splashing against the boulders, the whitewater areas of turbulence, the wave highlights, and the little C-shapes that show motion in calm water. Finally, highlight the tops of the foreground boulders with Titanium White.

Floral Still Lifes

Mums in Copper

Color Mixes

1. Raw Sienna
2. Burnt Sienna
3. Titanium White
4. Dark Brown
5. Dark Purple-Blue
6. Teal Blue
7. Dark Blue
8. Copper
9. Dark Copper
10. Light Yellow
11. Deep Gold
12. Medium Yellow
13. Butter Yellow
14. Light Butter Yellow
15. Warm Yellow
16. Cool Yellow
17. Very Dark Green
18. Leaf Green
19. Highlight Green

1 Lightly pencil in the line of the tabletop, the shape of the copper planter, and the mums. Using a spray bottle of clean water, lightly mist the surface to dampen. Wash in Raw Sienna in the top area above the table line. Glaze over this wash with Burnt Sienna. Soften and lighten the top right and lower right with Titanium White. Use Dark Brown to shadow and set back the bottom left. For the blue table area, wash with Dark Purple-Blue, using the edge of the sponge to draw a clean horizontal line. Accent the middle area with Teal Blue and shadow the left side with Dark Blue.

2   Block in the shiny copper planter with Copper, using the edge of the sponge to draw in the shape, and filling in with the flat of the sponge. With Dark Copper, draw in the rim detail and the shape of the feet, and shade the planter to create roundness. The reflection of the yellow mum on the rim of the planter is painted with Light Yellow and outlined with Titanium White.

3   Start the mums by blocking in their shapes with Deep Gold. Use Burnt Sienna to indicate flower petals on the background mums and highlight with Light Yellow. Paint petals on the larger, forward-facing mums with Medium Yellow. Go back to the background mums and highlight them with petals of Titanium White. Block in the right side mums with Butter Yellow and highlight with Light Butter Yellow. Go back to the forward-facing mums and highlight them with petals of Titanium White. Block in the middle mums with Warm Yellow and highlight with Cool Yellow. Go back to the right side mums and highlight them with petals of Titanium White. All the highlighting is done with an impasto technique to create some texture in the petals. Dot all the mum centers with Deep Gold. Use Very Dark Green to add stems and leaves. Highlight with Leaf Green, and add the final highlight to the leaves with Highlight Green.

Roses in Ebony

Color Mixes

1 Light Blue
2 Raw Umber
3 Yellow
4 Light Umber
5 Cream
6 Titanium White
7 Dark Gray
8 Dark Umber
9 Dark Leaf Green
10 Medium Leaf Green
11 Lightest Leaf Green
12 Dark Rose
13 Bright Red
14 Medium Red Rose
15 Rose Pink
16 Highlight Pink

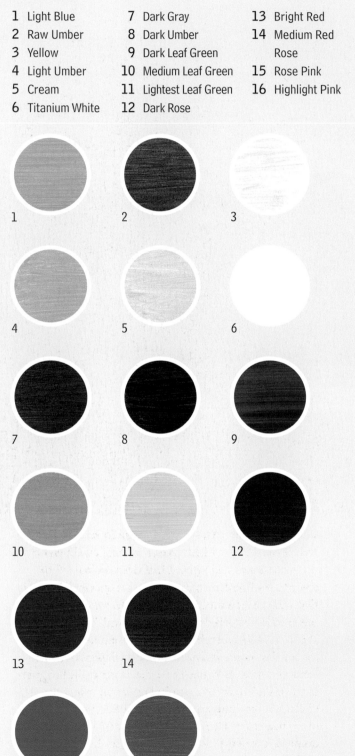

1 Lightly pencil in the round tabletop, the cylindrical vase and the roses. Using a spray bottle of clean water, lightly mist the surface to dampen. Wash in the background color above the table line with a Light Blue undercolor. Wash in the table top with Raw Umber. Dry-sponge Yellow over the blue background color in random directions, allowing the blue to show through in many areas. On the table top, dry-sponge Light Umber in random directions.

2 Mottle in a few areas of Cream over the blue/yellow background, and also over the tabletop. Mottle in some Titanium White over the tabletop, and add a cast shadow from the vase with Dark Gray. Block in the ebony glass vase with Dark Umber, leaving streaks of the background color showing through. Add streaks of Titanium White for a reflection, and soften the edges. Strengthen some of the white mottling on the tabletop.

3 Working wet-into-wet, sponge-paint the leaves with Dark Leaf Green for the darkest leaves, Medium Leaf Green for the lighter leaves, and Lightest Leaf Green for the yellow-green leaves. The darkest roses in the bouquet and the ones that are in shadow are blocked in with Dark Rose. Then their petals are stroked in wet-into-wet with Titanium White and a bit of Bright Red. Use Medium Red Rose to shape a few more roses, and stroke in their petals wet-into-wet with Titanium White. The lightest roses in the bouquet are Rose Pink, with petals stroked in wet-into-wet with white. Add rose buds on some of the outer stems with any of the rose colors. Come back in with Dark Leaf Green to overlap some of the roses with leaves to set them back. Highlight some of the roses with Highlight Pink and accent others with Bright Red.

Bouquet in Bronze

Color Mixes

1 Olive Green	8 Bright Red	16 Dark Leaf Green
2 Dark Brown	9 Deep Magenta	17 Medium Leaf Green
3 Black	10 Deep Red	18 Light Leaf Green
4 Deep Yellow	11 Bronze	19 Deep Salmon
5 Light Aqua	12 Raw Sienna	20 Delphinium Blue
6 Delphinium Undercolor	13 Black-Bronze	
7 Light Magenta	14 White-Bronze	
	15 Titanium White	

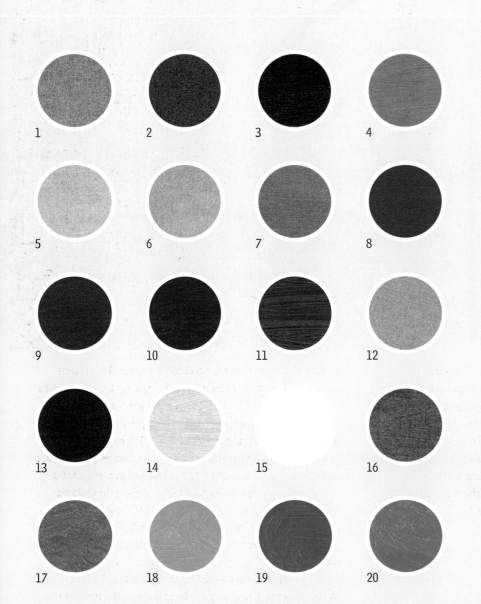

1 Lightly pencil in the line of the tabletop, the urn and the flowers. Mottle in the background color above the table with Olive Green, then Dark Brown. Wash in the tabletop with thinned Dark Brown, then marble with Black using the edge of the sponge to draw marbling lines. Block in the flower shapes with Deep Yellow, Light Aqua, Delphinium Undercolor, Light Magenta, Bright Red, Deep Magenta and Deep Red. The urn is blocked in with a solid wash of Bronze, and the initial details are delineated by lifting color with the clean side of the sponge.

2 Glaze thinned Raw Sienna over the background to warm up the colors. Shade the bronze urn with Black-Bronze in the shadow areas, then reinstate the details and highlight with White-Bronze. Use Black to shadow the marbletop table underneath the urn and around the base, and to re-establish the straight edgeline of the back of the tabletop. With Titanium White, establish the front and side edges of the tabletop, softening the line and blending into the top. Shade the front side of the tabletop with thinned Black.

3 Begin painting the leaves and stems with Dark Leaf Green. Add more leaves with Medium Leaf Green and highlight with Light Leaf Green. All the flowers are painted wet-into-wet. Reapply the same base colors used in step 1, then add the mid-values and highlights to each color. Highlight the Light Magenta flowers at left and the Bright Red flower in the center with Titanium White. Shade the Bright Red flower near the urn with Deep Salmon, highlight with white. Highlight the Deep Magenta flowers with white, and the Deep Yellow flowers with Deep Salmon. Over the Delphinium Undercolor, paint a second layer of petals with Delphinium Blue, highlight with white. Highlight the Light Aqua flowers with white. These are white flowers—the Light Aqua is the shading in the inner parts. To finish, place large leaves at the front and around the bouquet with Dark Leaf Green and Light Leaf Green. These will overlap the flowers and set them back.

tips for displaying your murals

✳ Murals are a fun and creative way to enhance your home. No matter what style of decorating you like, there are ways to display your mural that will fit right in with your tastes and budget. Here are three examples of display ideas for a range of decorating styles, from casual to formal to traditional, with helpful tips on how to achieve the look you like.

Mural may be painted directly on the wall. Or it may be painted on canvas and attached to the wall with wallpaper paste.

Buy door or window trim molding at a home center and paint it white or a coordinating color.

Miter the corners and nail or glue the trim molding to the wall, overlapping the edge of the mural slightly.

Instead of a piece of trim molding along the bottom, try attaching a simple plate rail or shelf with brackets for displaying items that play up the theme of the mural. For this beach scene, display bottles of sand, a starfish and a shell.

A mural can be an attractive addition to a paneled office or library, and can be displayed instead of, or along with, framed artwork.

Half-round wooden molding painted the same color as the walls gives a paneled look without the expense of real wood paneling.

Miter the corners and attach with a brad nailer or glue.

Attach molding over the edge of the mural to cover.

If you prefer not to attach a mural to your wall, here's an attractive and stylish alternative.

Allow enough room at the top to form a rod pocket along the back. Choose a rod and finials that coordinate with the mural's subject matter and colors. Slip the rod through the pocket and attach the finials. Attach brackets to the wall to hold the rod.

Decorate the rod with silk tassles, cording or beading for a touch of elegance.

Index

The best in home decorating instruction and inspiration is from North Light Books!

Decorative Mini Murals You Can Paint

Add drama to any room in your home with one of these eleven delightful mini-murals! They're perfect when you don't have the time or the experience to tackle a whole wall. You'll learn exactly which colors and brushes to use. And there are handy tips and mini-demos on how to get that realistic "wow" effect mural painters love. Detailed templates, photos and instructions ensure your success at every step.

ISBN 1-58180-145-9, paperback, 144 pages, #31891-K

Painter's Quick Reference Trees & Foliage

Fast instruction and inspiration is at your fingertips with Painter's Quick Reference: Trees & Foliage. You'll discover a comprehensive collection of easy-to-paint trees, shrubs, leaves, grasses, and distant foliage to inspire your work. With over 350 color photos and step-by-step instructions, this handy reference will give you the painting help you need... fast!

ISBN 1-58180-613-2, paperback, 128 pages, # 33183-K

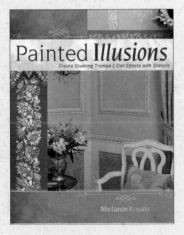

Painted Illusions Create Stunning Trompe L'oeil Effects with Stencils

Add incredible beauty and elegance to your home with *Painted Illusions*. Even if you've never painted before, you can achieve professional-quality results with these simple stencil techniques and Melanie Royals' easy-to-follow direction. In 19 step-by-step projects, you'll learn to create beautiful wall finishes that mimic fabrics such as linen, silk and damask as well as trompe l'oeil effects such as leather, porcelain, oak paneling, granite, carved stone, and more.

ISBN 1-58180-548-9, paperback, 128 pages, # 32899-K

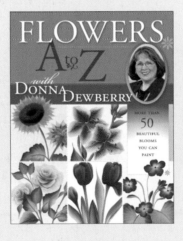

Flowers A to Z with Donna Dewberry

Painting your favorite flowers is easy and fun with Donna Dewberry's popular one-stroke technique! You'll see how to paint more than 50 garden flowers and wildflowers in an array of stunning colors. Discover Donna's secrets for painting leaves, vines, foliage, flower petals, blossoms, and floral bouquets. Add beauty and elegance to any project including furniture, walls, pottery, birdbaths and more!

ISBN 1-58180-484-9, paperback, 144 pages, #32803-K

These books and other fine North Light titles are available at your local arts & crafts retailer, bookstore, online supplier or by calling 1-800-448-0915 in North America or 0870 2200220 in the United Kingdom.